Unanswered PRAYER

A Mother's Treasury of Wisdom

SAREPTA HENRY

REVIEW AND HERALD® PUBLISHING ASSOCIATION
HAGERSTOWN, MD 21740

Originally published in 1910. Revised edition copyright © 2002 by
Review and Herald® Publishing Association

This book was
Edited by Raymond H. Woolsey
Copyedited by Jocelyn Fay and James Cavil
Designed by Tina M. Ivany
Electronic makeup by Shirley M. Bolivar
Cover photo by PhotoDisc
Typeset: Stempel Schneidler 11/13.5

PRINTED IN U.S.A.

06 05 04 03 02   5 4 3 2 1

R&H Cataloging Service
Henry, Sarepta Myrenda Irish, 1839-1900
    Unanswered prayer: a mother's treasury of wisdom.

    1. Religious life.   2. Christian life.   3. Children—Religious life.
I. Title

                        248.8

ISBN 0-8280-1649-6

To order additional copies of *The Unanswered Prayer,*
by Sarepta Henry, call 1-800-765-6955.
Visit us at www.reviewandherald.com for information on
other Review and Herald® products.

Dedication

To my children,
who have evidently entered into
a conspiracy
to save me from the consequences
of my own failures,
this little book
is lovingly dedicated
by their mother.

A Note From the Publisher . . .

When we rediscovered *The Unanswered Prayer* in our archives, we were amazed that though this book was first published in 1910, the commonsense advice it contains is as sound and practical as the most current child development resource. Mrs. Henry advocates teaching children how to exercise their freedom of choice in such wise ways that by age 12 they are equipped to make their way in the world.

Sarepta Myrenda Irish Henry never planned to be a leader or to change the world. A wispy young widow with fragile health, she wanted only to raise her three small children and share her love for God in her little corner of the globe. When the horrors of the liquor trade caught her attention, however, Sarepta became a formidable advocate for the temperance movement and eventually for the cause of organizing women within the Seventh-day Adventist Church.

She was a godly woman of lofty purpose, outstanding ability, and rare experience in public work. She was of the stuff that reformers are made, and of those few in the world to whom have been given an absorbing passion for souls. Her life reached out and touched countless thousands of people.

The brilliant and brief ministry of Mrs. Henry in the late 1890s officially launched the young Seventh-day Adventist denomination's program of "woman ministry." Her many books, pamphlets, and articles helped focus deserved attention on the Holy Spirit's gifts to women members of the church.

Before her untimely death in 1900 she had been a

well-known public personality virgorously involved in the anti-liquor campaigns of the era. She had been a national evangelist for the Woman's Christian Temperance Union before her 1896 conversion to Seventh-day Adventism.

For additional information on Mrs. Henry, read Margaret Rossiter White-Thiele's fascinating true story of her grandmother in *Whirlwind of the Lord* (Review and Herald Publishing Association, 1-800-765-6955; www.reviewandherald.com).

Chapter 1

ONE evening about 10 years ago, after I had spoken on the assurances of faith as the ground of hope in the temperance work, among others who came to speak to me was a woman whose appearance, from the first, fascinated me. She was standing near the door of the church as if she had paused in the act of exiting, and was looking at me as I stood near the pulpit. When our eyes met she turned and came slowly toward me. She was tall and walked with a stately carriage, and yet gave me the impression that she was not sure of her footing. Her hands were crossed at her waist over a black shawl that hung limply at either side. Her face was very pale, but at the first glance I thought, *That is a sweet, motherly face, the face of a Christian woman—a woman of faith and works, one who has entertained ministers, built churches.* But as she came nearer, I thought, *What is it that has overwritten all this with suspicion and distrust, and blotted out so suddenly the first flash of sweetness in that face?*

As she approached, I extended my hand; she took it in both of hers and said, "Tell me, truly, do you honestly believe that God hears and answers prayer?"

"Why, my dear woman," I replied, "of course I do! I could not have stood in this place and spoken the things that I have said tonight if I did not believe *that.*"

"Well, then," she said, with a defiant uplifting of her head and a steely ring to her voice, "why is it that in spite of the fact that I prayed for my only child, *my boy,* as long as he lived, from the day he was born, he lies tonight in a drunkard's grave? Answer me."

I was startled, and dumb. It was like a blow in the face, from which I recoiled. I had been engaged in reform work, had given the pledge of abstinence from alcohol to a great many people, and had learned from the talks that accompanied it that a great majority of them had come out of Christian homes. I had come to expect that such people would say to me: "I had just as good a mother as ever a person had. I was brought up in the church and Sabbath school." And from this fact I came to two conclusions: first, that in spite of the best of training, people would go astray; and second, that the prayers of the mother, the influences of the home and its pure love, would win them back somehow—and that the WCTU (Women's Christian Temperance Union) was the agent to be employed for this home-bringing.

But that it would ever be possible for any Christian mother to pray for her child all his or her life and then stand at last beside that child's dishonored grave, with the heavens declaring the glory of God above her and the earth budding and blossoming and fruiting according to His Word beneath her, and be left between them alone and desolate, in the terrible company of such a question as this—a question that must mock her love and faith forever—was something of which I had never dreamed. I was hundreds of miles from my own two boys, and it is safe to say that never before had I felt such a pang of homesickness as suddenly swept over me. I thought, *Can I do more than this woman has done? Can such a question ever stare me out of countenance as it does here?*

But she was waiting for my reply, and after a moment of rapid, painful thought I said, "I cannot answer you; I do not know how. I cannot imagine the reason for such a thing. Your question has taken me by surprise, for I never thought of such a possibility. But one thing I am sure I can say, on the spur of the moment, that wherever the failure is, it is not with *God*. More than that I cannot say, but I will find out. I will investigate and study. I will make it my one business to find an answer to your question, and sometime it may be that I shall meet you again and be able to say something more about it."

She pressed my hand closely in hers, gazed up into my face for what seemed a full minute, with a look that I shall never forget, and then, with a deep-drawn sigh and a "Thank you," she dropped my hand and turned away She walked down the aisle with the same lofty yet hesitating step, as if the foundations of the floor were weak under her feet. I never saw her in bodily form again. But she lives before me. She comes in with audiences. I never stand after an evening lecture at the altar of a church, with a sweeping gallery, a red carpet, and a broad aisle down the center, but I see that woman with the burden of that unanswered prayer upon her coming toward me. She intrudes upon the quiet of my study at home; she often stands before me, looking at me when I bow in my own room to pray, and she has been among the inspirations of the search that results in this little volume.

Had I chosen to forget my promise to her I could not have done it. I have been compelled to observe, as I have gone up and down in the land and out and in among the people, with reference to this subject. I have been compelled to study men and women and children everywhere; habits, laws of heredity, and life, and health, and disease; the promises of God and their conditions, the promises of parents and their consequences; young men and women, and social relations with their bearing upon the children of the future; doctrines, birth, and the *new* birth; the compass of the atonement of Christ, the power of the Holy Spirit; homes—kitchen, parlor, nursery, bedrooms, playgrounds;

schools—public, private, collegiate, church, and secular; my own failures, and those of other people. Scarcely a page has been read, or an object or social question that had intimate relation to human life been considered, without some thought of this, which has become to me the problem of this generation. It has been growing in importance day by day until it seems to cover everything else, and in itself to hold the key to the situation. It is the strategic point of the battle. It is the pivotal point of all effort for the better laws, and better society, and better religion of our hope. If we can find out *why* the boy was ruined, *why* the girl went astray in spite of all the praying of home and church, we shall know how to prevent a repetition of this greatest human disaster.

That there is need of a general awakening to the facts about us, no thoughtful man or woman can doubt. That woman is not the only one who is today asking this terrible question of God and the church. It has been dropped in one form or another into question boxes and has come in letters.

One morning I was called away from the breakfast table to meet an old man who asked to see me just a moment.

As I entered the room where he was waiting, he arose and said, "Pardon me, but I came because I thought you might help us. We have not slept all night: Mother is almost heartbroken at home. I could not wait for a seasonable hour. You have had experience—can you tell us how to save our boy? He is going to ruin—and why is it? We pray for him, we try to do our duty by him, but somehow he is going to ruin in spite of it all."

One evening, at the close of a lecture on this very subject, an old man arose in the audience and, asking permission to say a few words, exclaimed with every manifestation of deep feeling, "Why did you not come 40 years ago to tell us these things? It's too late for me, for my children have all gone to ruin." Then followed from this old man an appeal to young parents, especially fathers, that melted the audience as no words of mine had been able to do.

I had been repeatedly to a Northern town in the lumber regions, doing gospel work among drinking men, but we learned by sad experience how uncertain were the results of this work. Upon each return to the place, I was met by tales of terrible failure upon the part of the pledged men, and we began to look about anxiously for the cause. After a while, it seemed by common consent to be located in a house of bad repute kept by one whom they called Old Mag.

"Have you ever tried to reach her?" I asked of the women who were telling me the facts.

"You don't know Old Mag or you would not think of such a thing" was the reply, and the matter was dropped for the time, only, however, to come up again in the form of lamentations at the hopelessness of the work because of her terrible influence.

At a subsequent visit, upon inquiring about this woman I was informed that she was sick. "Then," said I to my host, "I must go to see her."

"It is hopeless, and scarcely safe" was the reply. She was in a house in a lonely place, adjacent to a bar and gambling hall of the worst character, utterly unfit and unsafe for respectable women to approach. But as we talked about it, the interest that had been from the first associated with her name in my mind grew to deep, restless anxiety. I could not be satisfied with anything until I had gone, so I signified again my settled purpose to make the visit if I had to go alone.

My host, the president of the local WCTU chapter, a lady of wealth and of great tenderness of heart, said that if I went she must accompany me, but that the consent of her husband must first be obtained. We approached him on the matter with much timidity; but after a moment of thoughtful silence, with something in his face that revealed the Christian heart within him as I had not before seen it, he consented and said that he thought it the right thing for some Christian woman to do. He added that it might as well be us as anyone to make the visit.

So we went together and found the place, as had been reported, in a most forbidding locality. We were directed to the room where the sick woman was lying. As we entered I was surprised to find, instead of an *Old Mag,* a very beautiful woman of not more than 35 years. The face that looked up at us from the pillow could not easily be reconciled with the things that had been reported of her. At first I thought there must be a mistake, but we soon found that she was the object of our search.

A startled look came into her large dark eyes as she recognized my companion, and then turned inquiringly toward me.

"This is a lady," said my host, "who has been trying to do us good in our city, and she wanted to come to see you."

The large eyes rolled up at me as I approached the bed and took the hand that lay outside the blanket, and the lips that quivered just a little in spite of themselves said slowly, "What did you want to come to see me for?"

"Because I have good news for you."

"For me—good news?"

"Yes, for you, *good* news—'For God so loved the world, that he gave his only begotten Son, that whosoever believeth in him should not perish, but have everlasting life.' 'This is a faithful saying, and worthy of all acceptation, that Christ Jesus came into the world to save sinners; of whom I am chief.'

"'Come now, and let us reason together,'" I went on. "'Though your sins be as scarlet, they shall be as white as snow; though they be red like crimson, they shall be as wool.'"

She had looked intently into my face as I said these words, her countenance changing and growing paler every moment, until at last with a sudden flush and a passionate cry she exclaimed, "That's not for me!"

"Yes, for you."

"No—no—no!"

"Why not for you?"

"Oh, I am *such* a sinner!"

"Well, *that* is just what gives you a claim on all this. It is because you are a sinner that you have any right to Christ and His promises."

"But you don't know—and I know all you can say! Oh, I know it all!"

"You do? How?"

"Oh, I heard it always at home. Who am I? Listen, I'll tell you a story. I am the only child of a Presbyterian minister, in the city of ———— would be impossible for any but a soul in just such agony to reproduce that cry.

Then followed the story—not that day; it was a continued story, all of which was never told, but from it were gathered many points that appear in this volume. Suffice it to say now that Maggie, as she was called from this time, was taken to a decent home and given a chance to get ready for the great change that was coming. Surrounded by the tenderest sympathetic influences, she passed away after a few weeks, taking her true name with her unrevealed, but leaving behind a testimony that gave us hope for her eternity. If we should go on and gather together the records of this work of ruin, typewriters and presses would grow sick under the heartrending task, and libraries would become as sepulchers of dead hopes for which there waits no resurrection. When such things can be, it behooves us to hasten to find the cause and the remedy.

Chapter 2

*I*N searching for light upon this subject of why good children go wrong, I have nowhere found any reason to revise my first statement to the woman mentioned at the beginning of the previous chapter. I have not found that the failure is with God, nor have I lost confidence in the mission of the Christian home. The home was the first institution that God organized. When He gave it its work to do, and consecrated it, He made ample appropriations out of the resources of His government for its success.

A good mechanical engineer, in building a motor or machine, makes careful estimate of all necessary friction and provides to overcome it, and leaves power enough to do the work. So with God. He was not unmindful concerning stimuli in the world outside the home, or the evil heredity that would threaten to defeat the home in its mission. He took into account the bar on the corner, the gambling parlor, the brothel, the inherited appetites for tobacco, alcohol, and immorality. All things were put into the scale and weighed over against the weakness of man and the power of God, and the appropriation was to be commensurate with the utmost need.

God's purpose was to have men and women who should be strong enough in body, soul, and spirit to go out and take the world as they should find it, and overcome it; to have dominion over it instead of being overcome or dominated by it. It was never intended that these sons and daughters should fall prey to any temptation that the world, the flesh, or the devil could bring against them. That they succumb is a sorrowful surprise to all the world as well as to heaven. Ruin in a Christian home is shocking because it is so out of the natural order of things. It is so much less than natural as to amount to deformity, just as the development of a beautiful, strong character in the midst of vicious or irreligious surroundings seems miraculous.

But although unnatural, so widespread is the terrible disaster that it behooves us to lay aside every selfish consideration and look the facts in the face with the utmost frankness. We must be willing to come to a fair understanding as to the methods of preservation. In inviting people to look at this question, I am aware that there has been left no place for it on the program of life—private, social, or public—and that it must be crowded in, so to speak. But I dare assume for it the importance that would warrant the suspension of everything else until the claims of the lives we have invoked shall have been settled, fairly to them, satisfactorily to God.

The failure may have been in the beginning of the little life; when such is the case, the only hope is in the help of God. Even in Christian homes there is a strange lack of appreciation of the responsibilities of parentage, and even in such homes is found a criminal disregard of the sanctity of human life.

Let us open the doors of one of the first houses we come to. It is furnished with the usual appliances of the ordinary Christian home. There are the piano perhaps, the bookshelves well filled, an assortment of magazines and papers, books of art, bric-a-brac. The cozy living room, arranged with an eye to effect in all its pretty details, speaks of the refined taste that presides over the domestic life of the average American. Upon the table lies the family Bible, open, for it is read once a day, at least. Upon the mantel stands a decorated cigar case—a gift from the wife to her

husband on his latest birthday. Of course he smokes—
why should he not? His father did before him, his pastor
does today. The elders, deacons, and Bible class leaders of
his church sell the weed in all its forms, along with the
family groceries. He, the young husband, acquired the
"manly" art in the natural way and has never thought anything about it, only that it was very cozy to have his own
sweet little home to smoke in, and his dear little wife for
his companion instead of the fellows of his bachelor days.

And his wife may not say a word for the world about
his smoking. Oh, no! She rather likes the odor of a good
cigar in the open air, only she sometimes wonders why
young men must always make the indoor air so heavy for
women to breathe, why a headache must, almost in-
evitably, follow her husband's homecoming. But she has
never thought much about it, and she has resolved to keep
young and lovely, and to make home the dearest place in
the world for him. Of course she has nothing to fear, for
he is a church member and even works with the youth of
the church; but she would not have him driven away with
his cigar for the world, for you never can tell just what
might happen in such a case.

The prenatal effects of the tobacco indulgence deserve
our careful, honest attention. The effect upon the nervous
system of the mother, as she is compelled to inhale all the
night, if not by day, the nicotine poison as it is emitted
with every respiration and heartbeat from the person of
the husband at her side, is in itself enough to rob her child
of a fair chance in the world. And when to this is added
the inheritance that has been transmitted through generations of a tobacco-using ancestry, each growing in its turn
shorter, more slight, more nervous, more impure as to
blood, less vital, less brainy, less muscular, what wonder
if the newcomer into this world of temptation finds him-

self or herself shorn of the elements of strength, by which alone they can hope to make a good fight against the enemies of purity! What wonder if the child ignominiously surrenders to the demon of appetite at the very outset and never gets in this life a good look at victory!

And when there are added to this the disorders, physical and moral, that the use of alcohol by the mother must induce in the developing child; when the mother's blood, in prenatal circulation, fills the child's veins with the fires of the alcohol thirst, and the mother's milk, from the first time that the child is taken to her breast, fosters the demon so that it grows with the growth of the child, we have a condition of things that to the eye that has been opened to see may well seem almost hopeless. And it would be hopeless had it not been written and verified that Jesus came into this world, into the place of demons and tombs, for such a need as this.

If this page falls into the hand of any man or woman who has been raised in just such circumstances and who knows the dark shadows of this hopeless, reckless despair, let me add that even to you there are given "exceeding great and precious promises: that by these ye might be partakers of the divine nature, having escaped the corruption that is in the world through lust [perverted appetite]."

By the substitution of this divine nature within us for the old poisoned humanity, there is salvation from the inherited and acquired lusts of the flesh, and by no other means.

And if these utterances just written, and the others that would flow from my pen, shall fall under the eye of some person such as the dear temperance advocate in whose home I am at this present date, who has stood aghast before me as I told her what calls forth this book; one who like her can say, "I never in my life heard of such doings! I do not comprehend your meaning"; I would ask that you take up a serious study of these social and domestic problems. Thus the strength of the pure thinking of a lifetime may be given to the work of helping to lift people out of the slums into which they have fallen. Also, pay close attention to the children growing up about you, for under the shadow of ignorance the most unclean things grow and increase.

Chapter 3

*I*N touching upon these domestic questions, we have to do with a great variety of homes, even among the class known as Christian. Among these, that one in which the mother stands alone for the defense of the truth and must do all the teaching alone calls for deep and tender sympathy. It may be that this woman was left to marry without any real knowledge concerning what marriage involved, with no preparation whatever for the real duties of wife and mother.

And her spouse may have been even less fit for his part in the domestic plan. Before marriage he may have had more of the kind of knowledge that means death than any memory can carry and ever hope for purity. The young mother must awake to the prospect of certain ruin for their child unless in some way the new life can be turned from the channels of the father's influence. The only hope for many a boy or girl in this life is that they may be preserved from the example of the father. Many are the women who are struggling with the energy of desperation to solve the problem of purity and truth for their children; many have given up in despair, and said, as one woman did to me, "It is useless for me to try to do anything for my children, for their father is against me. He says they are his as well as mine, and that they can do as he does if they want to."

This meant that they could use tobacco and alcohol, visit bars and places of questionable amusement, swear, break the Sabbath, and deride the truth represented by the dispirited, heartbroken mother. And at last they can grow reckless and hopeless and faithless.

For multitudes of women it is too late to come to the truth that in the clearer light of this day is beginning to shine forth. But for those whose children are as yet unborn this little book has a message. One thing I firmly believe: The woman in whose heart the will of the Lord is, who will honestly give all the powers of her being to Him and will be taught by His truth in relation to the physical and social as well as the spiritual life of her child, shall be able to make a pure, true Christian man out of her son, a true woman out of her daughter, in spite of an evil heredity and the example and influence of a profligate father.

"I wish I dared believe that," said a trembling voice out of the midst of a mothers' meeting. "Tell us why you dare utter so grand a thing," demanded another. The whole teaching of the Bible concerning the relation between the mother, child, and God, leaves us nothing else to infer. Motherhood with its pains and perils and responsibilities would be a mockery if it were left for the father to spoil the life of the child, in spite of the consecration of the mother and the power of God.

But the consecration must be *real,* and the spirit of God must have a fair chance at leading into *all* truth. And *all* truth sweeps a wide range, as wide as the necessities of human life. It will take *all* truth to redeem from actual degradation the life of this and coming generations; truth in the dinner pot and the leisure hour as well as in the sermon and at the family altar; righteousness in domestic dealing; the application of the Sermon on the Mount to common affairs; and *that* because of the life from the root of God, which flows through all the ramifications of thought and expression.

The practical application of the command "And whatsoever ye do in word or deed, do all in the name of the Lord Jesus" (Col. 3:17) would settle the how of this great problem.

This question has to do with the church home that, by the circumstances of money, position, social duties, etc., is exposed to special dangers, through special class temptation. These homes are supposed to be securely guarded from everything coarse or vile—and it is always a source of astonishment when moral impurity begins to intrude upon the select family circle of high-toned, refined, elegant Christianity. But it comes, and the heartbreak under a silken corsage is just as hard to bear as under serge. As parents, irrespective of class or grade, we are left to our choice between two things: either more ruin or more righteousness.

A serious cause of weakness in the family life is in the failure to recognize the authority of God's Word. "Thus saith the Lord" was intended to be the end of controversy, but too often it proves to be but the beginning of contentions, evasion, and prevarication. I heard a gentleman who represented the bone and sinew of the church in his place contend that the teachings of Christ could not be *literally* applied in this age of the world; that they required *explaining* from the "at sight" interpretation of the wayfaring "fool" to make them practical.

This was stated in the presence of his children, a quick, bright, eager trio, all ears during the discussion. The eldest, a son of 16, concluded from his father's premise that if Christ should come again He would revise the Sermon on the Mount and occupy entirely different ground concerning the world and its affairs. Therefore, it is really necessary to have a new and broader code; that the Bible is old-fashioned and obsolete; that it is not true that He is "the same yesterday, and to day, and for ever."

The amazement of the father when this conclusion was stated in bold, boyish fashion, as the lad attempted to show that his own ideas fully coincided with his father's, can better be imagined than described. He was not prepared for such an application of his ideas by his son! He had simply been trying to defend his own position as a businessman, and as a citizen advocating high license against the thrust of the truth as it is in Christ. If he were really to walk right up to the line of the life of Christ as he himself professed it and apply spiritual truth to practical things, there must be a radical change in his entire life among men. He could not *afford* that. It meant to suffer "the loss of all things," and of course he did not see how it could be practical that "godliness is *profitable*" in a worldly sense, nor how "all things" *could* "work together for good." And as to doing business and conducting politics on the "basis of faith," no man in his senses would do that!

The whole tendency of the profession and practice, the reason and faith, of this representative Christian was to make the gospel seem to the quick intelligence and straightforward sense of his boy as a hoax. And yet he was almost a model husband and father and friend. But so far as the real effect of his religious life upon his children was concerned, he might better have been an open infidel.

Another grave mistake is in making the dictum of the parent the law of the home.

"*My* word is law in *my* house. *My* children never say *why* to me," said one father with a peculiar setting of his jaws and a flash of his eyes.

"Then when does God come into your house?" he was asked.

"Oh—as to that, of course!"

He could get no farther, for the first statement was too

terribly true; so true as to shut out all of the real God-father. The law of God should be the law of the home; and father, mother, and children should be considered alike accountable to Him and to Him alone for the manner in which they deal with each other. Happy is that home where God is the recognized Father; His word the end of controversy.

This confident, trustful recognition of God's law and supremacy can be possible only when there is a genuine surrender of the whole being to Him. Prenatal consecration means an honest giving to God in recognition of His right to inheritance in every new life. The laws of heredity are so blessed, and yet so terrible, that we cannot afford to ignore them. Their study reveals the fact that children receive more from parents, in that which gives the bent of character, before birth than ever afterward, and that, therefore, every son and daughter has a right to a holy conception—to birth into a home into which the kingdom of our Father has come. In that kind of home His will is done as the angels do it in heaven, that is, *just as well as they know how;* that is called *perfect* by Him who takes such loving cognizance of our frame, never asking more of us than He is able to bring forth out of hallowed dust.

$$Chapter\ 4$$

IN looking over the ground of parental failure, I have found it to lie chiefly in little things. In nearly all homes, the great evils that threaten the purity of child-hood are forestalled. The barricades are up against the gi-ants, and yet we are not safe; we must fence against the "little foxes."

This book has to do with trifles, things too insignifi-cant to be often noticed, and yet so mighty in their results as to make it the only wisdom to search for them as the scientist searches with a microscope for the disease germ that is too minute to be recognized except through the most powerful instruments. Our cause, like that one, is one of life or death.

Prominent in the list of minute evils is the *exposure of the child to the creatures of the dusk.*

A little boy has come into a busy home. Father and mother are both intent upon making a place for him in the big world; he must have as good an education and start in life as any boy ever had. To this end there must be money, and to acquire the needed fortune there must be application to business in the home as well as in the store, or shop, or office. So the child, after being duly installed and consecrated in the most approved way, is turned loose and allowed to run, finding his own sweet way over the threshold, into the yard, out to the street or alley. There he finds others of the same sort, some older, some younger; one or two are as innocent as he, but many have already become proficient in street lore. Intimacies spring up, attractions crowd upon the little novice.

At first the shades of evening drive him back inside the house, through God's agent, the child's natural fear of the dark, according to the wisely foreordained plan for his preservation. But he is taught indoors as well as out that it is not manly to be afraid of the dark. So the divine precaution is circumvented by human wisdom; the natural barrier to evil broken down, he goes out boldly, and lingers; and the cover of the dark is none too heavy to hide him and his associates. They practice the things that make them adept in vice before they have learned the meaning of virtue.

The instinct of fear planted in the human mind is just as truly of God as is the life itself. He intended that by this the little feet should be sent flying into the light and shelter and safety of the home from the unclean things that hide and breed under cover of the dark. It is not "manly" to be afraid of the dark, but the babe is not yet a man; and the things that wait for him out there are so evil that the stoutest parent has reason to fear them for his child.

If this page falls open in the hand of any father or mother whose child *is not afraid,* and goes out "bravely, anywhere, after dark," and often has to be sought and brought home, allow just a personal suggestion. If you have never thought about it and can see no cause for alarm in this trifling thing, it will be well for you to follow the little fellow at your earliest convenience and surprise him and his associates at their pastimes. If you do not find that which will cause your cheeks to burn and your ears to tingle, your experience will be different from that of many parents who have tried the experiment.

The child who has come to enjoy the associations of the world outside his own home after dark has already taken lessons in those things that will make a clean mem-

ory an impossibility forever. And an impure memory is
something that even the blood of Jesus does not cleanse.
Anything that takes children out in the evening is dangerous—even if it be a church-related activity. The habit of
coming in and sitting down for the evening at home
should be so early fixed in children that they will know no
other way to do.

There is no place like home and the shelter of mother-
love for a little child under any and all circumstances.
There is danger in the broadest daylight in the gathering
together of little folks to amuse themselves alone.
However it may have been in past generations, it is true in
this, that the ordinary associations of children, in neigh-
borhoods where they play without the oversight of some
careful guardian—not a hireling but mother, aunt, or elder
sister—that these associations, I repeat, are dangerous.

So widespread and terrible is the disease of impurity
among the children of even "good" church homes that
there seems no remedy but by a vigorous process of
"stamping out," by each mother keeping her own carefully
under her own eye.

But you say, "I must do my work; I can't give the time
to follow my child about." Then draw your child after you.
I believe that God intended that the mother should be the
best and most delightful companion of her little ones; and
if she is taught of Him, she will find the secret of this. The
child should share in the real life and work of the mother,
and in this primary school of its life receive the preparation
for the broader circuit of the father's activities, and the en-
terprise of the world. The training of the hands, feet, and
tongue can best begin in the round of common household
service, and the mother who finds no place for these beginnings in her housekeeping, who can't be bothered with
the hinderings but, despising the day of small helpings,

sends the restless feet and hands that only need to be taught *how,* out into the street or alley or to a neighbor's house, misses the very best out of her life as a mother.

More than 20 years ago I knew a little maid of 4 years who, with her tiny housekeeping things, helped in all the work of her mother. Her little broom and duster, scrubber and dishpans, and soft cloths on a low table, always kept company with the taller and larger appliances of the woman. When the beds were to be made, she went to one side for her part. If a pail of water was needed, she drew it. If fruit needed to be gathered and prepared, she had her share in it all, and the work actually accomplished by this little one, increasing by month and year, came to be an important factor in the economy of the home. As the work was mutually shared, so was the leisure; the afternoon nap, the hour for reading, the rides, the visiting. Everything was done by daylight; and when other children came, the same policy was continued with sons as well as daughters. One thing has always been noticed from that day until now: their home was attractive enough to hold them and to draw their friends to them within its doors.

"But," you say, "children should have the association of children outside the home." Certainly, for a fractional portion of the day; a *small* fraction. Childhood is, however, too important a period in a human life to be wasted, and except it is spent among conditions that produce the best and highest development, there is loss that cannot be afforded. All their associations with each other should be presided over by adults. Children are not safe teachers of each other. It will not cost as much time, labor, or money to create safe and culturing conditions about the child as it will to rescue him or her from pollution.

That the necessary opportunity for sport and contact with others of their kind may be afforded to the little people, let the mothers in a neighborhood or a given social circle combine for the purpose. Each mother can take her turn in playing host to the flock for an hour or two in the morning, giving herself up to the task of directing the recreation of the children. The kindergarten system has put us in the way of a practical solution of the question of safe and healthful association for little children outside of the home, and whenever this means can be provided, nothing more is required. But this need not in any sense interfere with the real duties of any true mother.

Chapter 5

ONE serious mistake, and one that gives rise to many evils, is the fact that there are in many homes two worlds—one for the "big folks" and another to which the children are banished. Between these two hemispheres there seems to be "a great gulf fixed," so that there is no passing from the one to the other. The children are expected to know their place and keep it—"not bother their elders."

Mother is too busy all day to go out of herself into the children's life, and when daddy comes home at night he is too tired. Many mothers have as part of the evening's care the duty of keeping the children out of the father's way.

I shall never forget a scene of which I was a forced witness.

It was a beautiful home, blessed with two "bitter-sweet" children. I always wondered at the strange blending of these two flavors in them, until it happened that the secret was revealed in an unexpected way. Let me sketch the scene, which will tell its own story:

Time: Early evening. Place: The hall at the door of the children's room. Characters: Mother and 6-year-old Maddie.

Mother *(in steady, quiet tones):* No, Maddie; you must go now into your own room, and have a good time with little brother and all your pretty things.

Maddie *(shrilly, positively):* I don't want my things; I want my daddy.

Mother: It is strange that this must come up again. You know how it is, Maddie. You must entertain Freddy with—why, just think, there's your music box, we'll wind it up; and all your beautiful things that Daddy has worked so hard to buy for you, and—

Maddie: I wish he hadn't! I don't want my box! It only diddles and dins. I want my daddy!

Mother: Well, you can't have him this evening, Maddie. Daddy's tired, and—

Maddie: Ain't he *ever* going to get rested?

Mother: There, now! For shame! That's not a pretty way to talk. And it is of no use for you to act this way. If you don't want your music box, there are the big new book of pictures, and the building blocks, and—

Maddie *(suddenly brightening through her tears and putting a hand on each of her mother's cheeks, coaxingly):* Well, then, Mommy, you come in and play with us.

Mother: No, you know Mommy can't do that; you know Daddy expects Mommy to spend the evening with him in the family room.

Maddie: And don't he ever 'spect Freddy and me?

Mother: Madeline! Stop this instant, or I will send you to bed.

(Silence, broken by angry sobbing for a second.)

Maddie *(suddenly changing her tactics and clutching her mother's shoulder, beseechingly):* I'm sorry Daddy's tired; but Mommy, I won't bother him. I won't speak or make a bit of noise; I'll be just as still!

Mother: Then what in the world do you want to go in for?

Maddie: Oh, I want just to take hold of his fingers, and—and put my hand on his face.

Mother: Oh, you silly! What earthly good could that do you? No, you do as I told you. Go into your own room and play with Freddy.

Maddie: Oh-Oh-Oh!

It was a scream such as only an outraged heart can

give—a scream that rang through the house as she went sorrowfully away.

What was Maddie's crime? She simply wanted bread and could not be put off with a stone; she longed to drink in love, out of the bright depths of her father's beautiful eyes; and no number of things that could "diddle and din"—that could squeak and squawk and almost talk—could meet the need of the hungry little heart. She had spent happy hours when her father gave himself to her; he was to her the very representative of that One among ten thousand, that One altogether lovely, and she could not spare him out of her life and yet grow up sweet and strong as she had been planned.

Into this world to which the children are banished come strange things that deserve our notice. Among them are questions of all sorts—"silly," "queer," "indecent" questions come from everywhere and about everything; springing up under foot, dropping from above, darting out from the secret of the little ego. The child cannot turn either way without being confronted by questions that must be answered. And of all annoyances in the average home, the question of the child is the most aggravating. Hence arises a problem upon the settlement of which depends much of weal or woe to all concerned.

One day, after a private lecture to mothers in which I had talked plainly, a woman asked, "What would you do if your boy came to you with an embarrassing question?"

"An embarrassing question?" I repeated.

"Why, yes; you know they will—" and she went on to explain that a few days before, she had entertained a company of ladies and gentlemen. As they sat together, her little boy rushed in with a question that brought the blush to every woman's cheek. "I was so ashamed and embarrassed," she said, "and would like to know what you would do in such a case."

"First," I said, "I would like you to tell me where you find any natural cause of embarrassment between a mother and her own son."

"Why," she said, with a look of disgust, "boys do ask such awful questions for a woman to answer."

" 'A woman'—the mother? To whom shall he go if not to you? Why not to you? Is not your son just as truly of your own body as your daughter? Are you not his natural teacher in all things that belong more especially and privately to his own life?"

Many are the mothers who, like this one, look with disgust on the child as he comes with the innocent frankness of first confidence, with the natural questions that should have been forestalled by pure, truthful teaching. An unanswered question is a terrible, often a deadly, thing for a child to carry away, with the accompanying sense of humiliation that results from the rebuff he has received. Suppose the mother is embarrassed and blushes at his question, or is horrified and turns him away with a rebuke or some evasion. Is the child answered? Will the blush satisfy him? Will it not rather be as a spur to curiosity, driving him out to find someone who will answer him?

"But," says some mother, "it is of no use. I cannot talk to my boy about such things."

Then you must take the risk of defilement for him. Unless his questions are truthfully and candidly answered, unless he is taught concerning all things that pertain to his life as a man, from the basis of God's Word and the pure standpoint of a consecrated home and a mother's love, he will learn from the tongue of vice and the standpoint of an unclean world. We have the choice of but two things: either to teach our children to think purely and truthfully of each unclean thing, or to leave them to be taught to think impurely of the most sacred things. Any boy who is worth having, who has in him the elements of real manhood, will not take embarrassment, even from his mother, as the solution of the problem. And that mother who sends her son or daughter to anyone else for the answer to a question that belongs essentially to personal life and natural relations loses the one grand opportunity of her life to bind her child to her with bonds so sound and strong that no unholy influence shall be able to break them.

It is the office of the mother to teach the son, as well as the daughter, the ethics of the body. There are a few men who have in them the *motherly sense,* so softening and sweetening and spiritualizing fatherhood, that they could be trusted with this delicate service for the little son; but they are more rare than century blossoms. Hence to the mother it has been given to bear this cross, as well as to wear the crown, that shall be hers as the reward of faithfulness to the questioner at her knee.

"How soon shall this teaching begin?" comes the inquiry. "How early will it be wise to open up the secrets of his own being to the innocent child?"

As fast as the questions come, at least before there is a possibility of any exchange of thought on this subject between the child and the outside world, its mind should be fortified by *facts* simply, delicately, and very plainly told. In the bath, in the hands of the mother, should the teaching begin.

"What should be taught then, and how?"

The child should be taught that the little body is built by God for the habitation of His Spirit, and that it is all good and sacred.

The evils of impurity and their widespread prevalence among children, even of so-called good homes, render necessary increased care upon the part of the mother if she would see her child grow up clean. Innocency must be clad in the armor of knowledge and be shod with discretion.

A mother who had been a teacher in a city school looked forward with dread to the day when her boy should be compelled to encounter the influences that haunted the playground and its environs. She thought about it day after day as the time approached, and devised various plans for keeping him away from this pestilential atmosphere. Sometimes she thought she would prefer that he should never be educated than to run the risk. But she knew she could not keep him out of the world. He had his life to live, his work to do, and he must begin in the school at its next opening. At first she thought she would have a talk with him and tell him that as he was going to school to learn, he would hear a great many new things, good and bad, and that he must distinguish between them. He must remember the good and profit by it, but forget the bad words and things that wicked children would like to teach him.

But she had no sooner thought this over than she saw she would be asking an impossibility of her boy to ask him to forget; and to ask an impossibility of her child was to lose her cause at once. So she changed her plan, and on the evening before he was to start to school, she said:

"Now, Bertie, you and I must make a bargain about these days when we are separated. You are going to school to learn the things that you cannot learn at home. You will learn from your teachers, and from other chil-dren, and from people on the street as you go to and from school. Some things will be good, some will be bad. Now, if you hear a word from a boy or a girl, or anyone, that you never heard me use, or if anyone gives you anything new, be sure to bring it home to me. As for me, I will re-member what I hear, and when we have our bedtime talk, we will tell each other all about it."

And so it was. The whole vocabulary of profanity and obscenity was brought to her by her boy. He would sit on the arm of her chair and, with his innocent eyes wide open into hers, utter with his sweet mouth the dreadful things he heard, while she was alternately burned and chilled by the emotions of indignation and shame and anger that washed over her. Sometimes it would seem that she must cry out, "Stop! Stop!" but she carefully guarded herself so that he should not be repelled or made to feel that he was doing wrong. And then she would "apply the sieve," as she called it, and tell him what was bad, and why. She left him nothing to seek after in the way of whys and wherefores, but made clean work as they went along with all that he brought in. And that mother had the satisfaction of seeing that son grow up with a clean tongue and a face marked by peculiar sweetness, strength, and purity of expression, passing through the fire without so much as the smell of it on his garments, to the place where the Spirit set him to preach His gospel.

The thoughtless practice of allowing children to sleep with others away from home is a fruitful source of crime against personal purity. Upon *no account* allow a child of another family to share your child's bed, and even in the same family it is better that each should have his own individual bed. Said a lady who had brought up a large family to be good and pure:

"The children of my neighbors had at first the common idea that to go and stay all night was the desirable way for a visit. They would come and ask for my children to spend the night with them until they found it was of no use. At last one little girl came to our home uninvited, and was shown into the guest bedroom to sleep alone. I think her consternation was the most pitifully comical thing I ever saw.

"'But I came to sleep with Sadie,' she said.

"'Oh, Sadie sleeps alone. At our house, company always sleeps here in the guest room.' It was more than the little one could endure, and it became our pleasant duty to take her home to bed."

The close contact of a common bed provides a rare chance for unnamed evils to work the ruin of the sweetest child.

There is nothing about words that will reveal themselves to a child, only as he is taught to apply them. Nor has the child any data from which to judge of any act, nor any experience from which to forecast consequences. Children are entirely dependent upon those among whom they live for all things that shall make for good or bad. Not long ago I heard some good people discussing a lad of a few years of age, who had never had any chance to know much that was good. It was said of him that he was "depravity personified," and the entire blame was laid upon him. But one who would stop to think and give candid recognition to facts would be obliged to confess that he was probably doing as nearly right, according to his knowledge, as the average man.

It is understood that children must be taught skill in the use of tools of all sorts; a child who can "pick up a trade" without an industrial education is always considered an anomaly. Years of application are required to train the intellect to correct methods of thinking; and yet the little legatees of generations of unholy living are judged and condemned because they are not able to do, in morals, that which none would presume to expect in art or science. The little untaught lips are expected to discern the flavor of an unclean word and reject it as they would tainted meat; and as for impulse and conduct, nothing but purity, gentleness, sweetness, must appear to the public eye. Children must know how to cater to the popular taste in what they present, or be repudiated at once.

Children untaught concerning the strange nature that they have inherited, with its appetites perverted into passions before they were born, driven out before the reticence of their busy mothers to the tutorage of the street, are yet expected to discriminate at sight against everything unchaste, and practice the purity of which they have been kept in ignorance, instead of the uncleanness which they have been diligently taught in the streets. They are expected to eschew the vile language of the world to which they have been banished and speak only the unknown tongue of culture and refinement; to obey the laws and respect the rights about which they have not even heard. And when the little man or woman, according to the spirit of the age, begins to improve on all they have been taught, and make it practical in their small affairs, their parents are shocked, the community is outraged, and they are outlawed. Many hardships and sorrows come into their young lives for which they can give no adequate reason. They have simply been acting as they have been trained—and why not? Why are they looked at askance? Why are they condemned? Or is that the way of the world? Oh, the pity of it! and the shame and the wrong! And how shall the little ones escape?

As I look upon these things I am more and more glad that Jesus said, "Suffer little children, and forbid them not, to come unto me: for of such is the kingdom of heaven," and I count those happy who escape early from a forbidding world into the sheltering arms of that blessed "Me."

Chapter 6

*T*HE money question weighs heavily in the scale of ruin or salvation of the youth. It is by money consecrated to holy service that under God the world is to be finally redeemed; and by money prostituted to vice it is being destroyed. So dangerous is this weapon that children should have the most careful training in its use. And yet in the majority of homes very little thought is given to the part that carelessly tossed nickels and dimes must play in the child's destiny. Three word-painted scenes will illustrate the point.

A young father stands for the first time with his first-born in his arms. His face is full of manly expression; one tiny hand is already clasped around his finger. "God helping me, I will be a true father to this boy; we will grow up together to be father and son; I will never break his clasp on me."

This purpose becomes the rule of life between the two, and it is a thing beautiful to see. Little John is his father's constant companion outside of business hours. About the house and yard he goes astride his father's tall shoulders, until long after his own legs are fully able to carry him.

John's father is a banker, and the little one is taught from the first that he is a part of his father's plan and business and is growing up to be his partner. The effect of all this upon the young life is like that of a strong, tall support to a climbing rose tree, lifting up and up all the thoughts and impulses of the child so that, without being precocious, he is yet more than a man-child while but an infant in years. He is growing up to go into business with his daddy; and Daddy says he is growing fast, so the time must soon come when he will be large enough.

"I'm 'most big enough, Daddy," he often cries out with delight, stretching up to the utmost.

"Getting big enough!" is the glad reply of the proud parent.

"I can go down to the bank and begin soon."

"It will not be very long."

And yet the child is in short pants.

At last there comes the wonderful day when, for the first time, John has long pants to put on, and to his mind this is all that has been lacking. A pair of long pants with pockets! Certainly he shall go to the bank today.

The proud father, unconscious of all that is in the mind of the child, feeds the hope of the little heart by sweet words and smiles—all quite misinterpreted by the boy. At last it is time for the father to say goodbye and get in the car for the commute to the city. The boy, dressed in his little overcoat and having no thought but of "business," walks proudly after his father to the car, and then learns that he is not yet considered big enough to go. He is too stouthearted to cry, and too strong-willed to let his father leave him behind without another effort to go with him. He throws two sturdy arms about the father's leg, clasps it tight, and holds on.

Father had said he would never break the clasp of his boy's hand upon him, but it looks very much as if he would be obliged to do so now, or miss the commute, or take John with him. But he has a happy thought. Taking a bright new quarter from his pocket, he hands it down toward the child, saying: "Here, John, this is a part of the bank. You shall be Daddy's little banker at home today.

You can help this money along into circulation. By and by Mommy will let you go down to the candy store and spend it. Here, we'll mark it so we will know it when it gets back to the bank again."

The bright spirit of the boy understands and responds. He loosens his clasp and takes the coin, along with a goodbye kiss from his father. The latter slams the door to his car and is off, leaving John to settle the rest of the affair with his mother.

We shall not be able to follow this particular quarter any farther, but another is on its way, which brings us to the second picture.

Time: About 8:30 on a summer morning. Place: Along a neighborhood street.

Two little fellows are just ahead of us. The younger boy moves his head in earnest talk about what he is going to do with the quarter that he holds between the thumb and forefinger of his right hand; the other hand clasps the hand of his companion.

The chatter of the children, their bright faces and graceful movements, interests us so much that we hesitate to hasten past, so we slacken our steps and loiter behind them. We learn from their animated remarks that "Daddy" had given the coin to the younger boy, and he is taking his older friend to the candy store to treat him—or rather, the older boy is taking the younger one and his money, for the older boy has become wise in the ways of the palace of sweets.

We are detained on the way for a moment, so that the children enter the store before we reach its door. But when we arrive and look in, we behold as pretty a tableau as one often sees. Five boys are standing in a row before the counter. One, about 9 years old, is at the farther end of the line, while our little men, with the younger at the end, are nearer the door. The child stands on tiptoe, looking up into the face of the candy man, who is beaming upon him. The quarter is lifted invitingly, trustingly, upward while the candy jars stand temptingly in their places.

We have just taken in the pretty group when the voice of the 9-year-old cries out shrilly, "Say, cigarettes is better'n candy!"

Immediately every face is turned toward the oracle, and our little boy has written all over his face in dimples and colors: *I know candy's good. If cigarettes are better, I want some.*

The candy man laughs and, seeing us at the door, nods toward the children as much as to say, "There is young America for you!"

Whether this quarter in the hand of this child can get cigarettes, we have no means of knowing, for they will not be brought forth as long as we are standing by. But there are places where they are waiting, along with all their vile concomitants of obscene pictures and texts for just such innocent, unwary hands.

And the child who has learned that "cigarettes is better'n candy" is already on the way to ruin—physical, mental, and spiritual.

Picture No. 3 introduces us to a clothing merchant. He has been a teacher in the city schools and is interested in growing children. We enter into conversation as we look at goods on his long counters. After we relate to him the foregoing incident, he replies, "I can more than match that," and proceeds to make his word good.

He relates: "One morning when I went to the rear of the store I heard voices outside—voices of children, not in play but steady talk, and quarrelsome. At last I began to investigate. At the back of the building there is a pile of cartons. The voices seemed to issue from one large box that was set with its open face toward the wall. I looked in, and there were three little fellows experimenting with a bottle of beer. I questioned them and found that they belonged to families who would not have believed their children knew what beer was. By some means they had been decoyed into spending money for the stuff and had been so well trained in keeping secrets that it was impossible for me to ascertain where they got it."

"Well, of course you at once told their parents," we remark.

"Ah!" he replies with a shrug. "I have cut an eyetooth."

"What do you mean by that?"

"Mean? Why, their parents are good customers of mine, and I do not intend to drive them away."

"Oh, I see! Who are these parents?"

"Oh!" with another shrug. "I have cut *two* eyeteeth."

This man's fear for his business makes him immovable in his determination that this that he has discovered shall not reach the parents or the bar owner through him.

Children left to experiment with money, in a world so grasping and unprincipled, are in danger. A thousand evil, covetous eyes are upon every coin and will get it out of the little fingers in exchange for any worthless thing. Before children are sent out alone to spend a penny there should be established between them and their home that relation of confidence that alone can preserve them from disaster. They do not know by instinct what things in the world's great market are bad. They go by the sight of the eye, the hearing of the ear, and the titillation of the palate, until they have been taught to let reason dominate their choice.

Every child should have a regular allowance of money, and then by the most painstaking care be taught its proper use and to keep an itemized account and report the same.

In any home where there is ordinary food and clothing, there is means enough to provide an allowance for each child. If not more than a dollar per month, let this be conscientiously paid over and, in exchange, require a careful statement at regular periods.

"But," said one mother, "how shall I know that my child makes a true statement?" That depends entirely upon what you gave your child, out of the secret of your own life. What you are before God, what you are to your child, will settle that. And this brings us back to the prenatal relation with its responsibilities, and to the individual consecration to God, which includes this hidden life, and to the strange, lonely world to which childhood is so often banished, and to the unanswered question. The manner in which the rights of the children are ignored makes them unreliable in word and deed. They are held responsible, but no one is supposed to be responsible to them, beyond convenience or pleasure. Promises to the child are broken with impunity; while if they break a promise they are severely dealt with.

Here is a case in point:

Jim was a 10-year-old lad on a Pennsylvania farm 40 years ago; a carefree, great-hearted boy, loving everything that was alive but with no taste for "chores."

One spring morning he discovered, to his great delight, a new colt in the pasture and at once desired it for his own. On his making his wish known, his father readily agreed that he should have the colt, upon condition that he would do his daily chores without being told.

"Honest?" cried Jim.

"Honest! If you will do this, we will say that you have earned him, and he shall be yours."

"All right, I'll do it." Jim's delight could be expressed only by a somersault.

"Well, we will see," said the father.

"Yes, you *will* see," replied Jim.

It took many months to demonstrate all that the boy meant by this exclamation, but the entire household was obliged to acknowledge that he was as good as his word. As time passed, all conceded that, according to the terms of the contract, the growing animal was Jim's own. The boy and horse were inseparable companions at all times when off duty. There was a place at the pasture fence where Prince learned to await his little master's coming from school, knowing full well that there would be a dainty bit of maple sugar or an apple for him to find in the wide pocket of Jim's jacket. Then would follow a happy gallop about the fields or a canter along the highway. Prince was always tame, never had to be broken to halter or bit or saddle, so perfect was the understanding between him and his little master.

One day, when Prince was about 3 years old and Jim 13, when the boy came from school he rushed as usual to the trysting place at the pasture fence, with pocket full. To his surprise, Prince was not in sight. He called, but no Prince came. Seeing his father at work about the barn, Jim ran to him and expressed his surprise at the unusual conduct of the animal in straying off after this fashion. He was coolly informed that a horse dealer had been along that day, and Prince had been sold.

"Sold!" cried the boy in astonishment.

"Why, yes, sold, of course."

"Sold! I never intended to sell Prince. Why, he—is—part—of the—family! I can't have him sold."

"Can't? Well, he is sold and gone."

Jim stood a moment, dumb with the shock of amazement; and then he made indignant protest, crying while he clinched his fist, "I'd like to know what right you had to sell him! He was *mine!*"

"Yours? Now, see here, Jim! The sooner you understand matters, the better. He was *yours* until *I* wanted him, just as everything else is. Your clothes, your time, your work, the money you will save, everything you have, is *mine* by law until you are 21."

"I don't see how! I don't believe it!" cried the child, too astounded to remember that he was speaking to his father. His father was willing to make him understand.

"Well, it is so, as any lawyer will tell you. You and all you have belong to me until you are of age. So now, stop your noise and go about your chores."

Then ensued a rebellion, in which the big man was victor for the time.

Jim went about the chores, but with surly mutterings.

His father, hearing these, called angrily after him, "Stop that muttering or I'll give you something more to mutter about."

Jim let his voice drop down to a scarcely audible tone, but he kept on saying, "Wait till I grow up! Wait'll I grow up! If he'd a'done it to anybody else he'd a'been a horse thief! He *is* a horse thief. A horse thief, a horse thief—a 'orse thief, 'orse thief! 'orse thief, thief, thief—f-f-f!"

From that time Jim would make faces, *inside,* when a blessing was asked at table or prayers were offered. He dragged himself about the chores, doing only what he was compelled to do. He cared nothing for his clothes. Why should he? They were not his but his father's, and his father had lots of money. He'd make him pay back in some way what he got for Prince. But at length, without waiting to grow up, he took destiny into his own hands and ran away. Neither father nor mother ever heard from him again.

Years after, Jim, grown to be one of the prosperous businessmen of the West, said to me, "It will be to me a lifelong regret that I did not know a better way out of the difficulty than to run away. My parents have gone beyond my reach, or I would hasten to ask their forgiveness for the sorrow I must have caused them. I did wrong, but I did not know how to do the right. But I made up my mind that my boys should profit by all that this taught me. I intend to deal by them as I expect them to deal by the rest of the world."

Over against this, let me set another father and son, in whom there is a lesson so sweet and pure that I turn to it with delight.

Several years ago I received a letter bearing a letter-head that I will call "Robert Smith & Co." It was written by Mr. Smith, who stated that he lived in a town that was infested with bars and near a penal institution. The churches seemed without power to stand against the terrible influences about them, and no temperance work was being done, though they all realized it was a bad place in which to bring up boys. He wished to have me come at my earliest convenience, to lecture on "What Is a Child Worth?" I named a date, and at the appointed time arrived in the little city. Mr. Smith awaited me and conveyed me to his home, where we arrived just in time for supper.

As we drove into the yard we were met by a fine specimen of boyhood, whom Mr. Smith introduced to me as "my son, Frank." There was something in his manner that made me feel that I was expected to treat Master Frank as if he were six feet high, and yet there was nothing about the boy of that offensive assumption that sometimes awaits only the slightest notice to call it forth. He greeted me with modest politeness and took my suitcase. I was strongly attracted by the noble, boyish face and his pleasant, busy ways as he moved about during the short time before we were to start for the courthouse, where the lecture was to be given.

There were two women visiting, and the family vehicle seated but four, so when we were ready to go Mr. Smith said to his wife, "You take the ladies; Frankie and I will walk. You will get there before us; wait at the corner until we come."

We arrived at the corner and sat and waited until Mrs. Smith began to grow nervous.

"We shall surely be late," she said again and again.

At length Mr. Smith and Frank came. "You know, dear," he said, "how it always is. I was stopped by So-and-so and lost precious time. We are late." He then gave Frank some minor assignment, with the comment that he would open the meeting and then come back for the boy.

We hastened into the hall, which was crowded. Chairs were brought in from other rooms, and much time was consumed. Mr. Smith had all the arrangements on his own hands, so that he became entirely absorbed in the service.

After the lecture he was introducing me to the people when Mrs. Smith came and asked, "Robert, where is Frankie?"

I do not think I ever saw anyone forget the civilities of life so quickly as did Mr. Smith. He dropped the introductions and hastened toward the door, followed by his wife; I followed after her.

At the door Mrs. Smith turned back for me, and we went on to the street corner together. We found Mr. Smith sitting on the curbing with Frankie in his arms, and Frankie was crying. It was in April. The evening was very chilly, and the boy had not prepared for the long standing in the open air. He was shivering, and as we came up he was saying, "Did you truly forget me, Daddy?"

"I am ashamed of it, my son, but I did," replied Mr. Smith, and then he went on to explain why, and to apologize as carefully as if it were a man instead of a boy whom he had forgotten. But at last, as if a sudden thought came to him, he asked, "But, Frank, what made you stand out here in the cold? Why didn't you just come inside?"

Then Frankie sat up, and turning his face to his father's, said, "Daddy, is that the way you and I do business?"

Nothing further was said. Mr. Smith looked up at his wife with a grave smile and, lifting Frankie from him a little, arose and began helping us into the car.

Upon reaching home, Mr. Smith and Frankie came into the room where Mrs. Smith and I were sitting by the fire.

"Excuse us, ladies," he said. "We have a little business to talk over while we get warm." He drew his armchair to the table. Frank found his seat upon his father's knee, then drawing forward a pile of letters and taking a pair of little scissors from his pocket, the boy began cutting the envelopes. He and his father read and talked together, until all had been discussed.

At last Mr. Smith arose, with the boy clinging, laughing, to him, with arms and legs coiled about him, and brought him to say goodnight to me and kiss his mother, after which they went away together. Mr. Smith was gone some time and returned alone.

Drawing his chair beside us, he turned to me and began talking about ordinary affairs. But I interrupted him, saying, "None of these things have any charm for me now; just one subject interests me, and that is Frankie Smith. I want to know about that boy."

"Well," he replied, with a pleasant laugh, "we think he is a pretty fine boy. You made your estimate none too high."

"Yes, I understand all about that, but there is something more. I want to know what all these things mean. Why did he wait out in the cold? What did he mean by the way you and he do business? I hope you understand me."

"Yes, I think I do," he replied, pleasantly but soberly, "and I am willing to explain everything. Frankie has just as much interest in my business—our business—as I do. Did you notice the letterhead on the letter I sent you—'Robert Smith & Co.'?"

"I did."

"Well, that 'Co.' is simply another way of spelling Frank Smith."

"Honestly?"

"Honest and true; I have no other partner."

"And he is practically your partner in business?"

"He is; just as practically as if he were 30 years old. I determined from the first that he should be associated with everything in my life. As he grew up a little, I thought I would tell him everything about my business that he could understand, and so, sometime, make him my partner. But after a while I saw that I had better tell him everything and leave him to indicate when he did not comprehend; and that I had better not wait for years to qualify him for partnership. Of course, his share is that of a *boy,* but as we operate it is just as valuable as my man's share. He makes his own little investments, does his share of the work, and there is not a thing about the premises that we do not own jointly. People here have come to understand this, also, and he is treated accordingly.

"His work is, of course, such as he can do out of school. This that you saw him do tonight is part of it. He takes and brings all the mail, opens all letters, files them away, and many he will answer as well as I. I leave him to meet a business engagement with men, not in my place, but in his own. He does not represent me, but our joint interest. We confer together about everything, his play as well as his work."

"And what do you propose to make of him?" I asked.

"A Christian businessman, unless, indeed, the Lord should want him to preach His gospel."

"And this in the very town that you wrote me was such a bad place in which to bring up boys?"

"Yes, here, for our home is here."

"And you are confident of success?"

"Surely, I am confident."

"Yes; and I see your plan. It commends itself to my judgment. But there are so many snares, so many failures. Please tell me in a sentence, if you can, how you expect to accomplish this grand result."

Mr. Smith sat in thought a moment, then said: "To put it all into one sentence, I should say this: I intend to keep my boy so close to me that there shall not be room for an unclean habit or an unholy association to come in between us. I think that covers my part of it. His mother has her work to do for him, which I cannot do, but I have my work, which she cannot do. I have always said I would not leave him to be brought up alone by his mother unless I was compelled to go away out of the world. In that case I know my wife would be equal to the emergency. But while I am here I propose to keep up my end of the responsibility.

"Now about his going to bed at night. Ever since he went out of our own room I have put him to bed. We always have our little private talk, our verse or two of Scripture, and prayer together. His mother and he have their confidential time in the morning, when she and he read a little together and pray. He and I are now going through Proverbs together, verse by verse. I leave nothing for him to wonder about. We had Romans last. Mother is taking him through John's Gospel now, I believe.

"I remember from my own boyhood something of what it is to have a father's help in Bible reading and prayer, and so we have this little arrangement. I intend never to forget that my boy is growing up to be a man and not a woman. I am confident that if I really do my part honestly, I can trust God to do His, and so among us all we shall get a good, true man out of this beginning."

"I believe you," I said, with my heart full to overflowing. "Under these conditions I believe it would be safe to match Frankie Smith against all the bars, gambling halls, and houses of sin in the land."

More fatherhood is needed in the home. While it is true that an unworthy father should not be allowed to entirely spoil the work of a mother for her son, or prevent the work of the Spirit of God for him, yet neither the mother nor God can do the work of the father, and the child who fails to secure it must always miss out of his life that which the father should have built in, from his own true and pure influence.

Chapter 7

THE literature that comes into the hands of our children has a controlling influence in shaping their future. From the fact that so much that is pernicious is afloat, and that children are left so much to themselves, the printing press has come to be not an unmixed blessing. Upon no question has the home been more asleep; upon none has the wicked world been more alert. Through the eye, directly to the heart and life, the corrupt stream has been flowing, until it is almost true that there is no place clean.

An incident from real life illustrates both the indifference and the need of alarm. I was called to conduct a WCTU institute and give a special lecture on social purity. The lecture was to be on Sabbath afternoon, while the institute occupied the preceding week. At an early day during the institute, after the announcement that I should speak on such a subject, a gentleman waited upon me, saying that he represented several others who had sent the request that I should not discuss that subject among them.

"Why not?" I asked.

"Because there is no need of it in our midst; no immorality of that sort."

"Then," I said, "you must truly be in the vestibule of Paradise."

"Well, we are a clean people," he said. "Our town is more than a century old, has been all the time under good government. We care about our youth. We know what comes to them, and we do not want this subject discussed to turn their thoughts in this direction."

"In what direction, pray?" I asked. "That of social purity? You may be sure their thoughts have been turned in the direction of social *im*purity."

"Oh, I am sure you are mistaken. We have carefully guarded all avenues and have kept our community untainted."

"I should be very glad to be convinced that this is true," I said, "but you will pardon me if, when you number bars by the dozen, I should be skeptical as to the purity of your city. Besides, I was especially called here by the organization of mothers to speak upon this subject, and cannot break my engagement with them at the instance of any other organization. If you do not wish the lecture that they have announced, your only way out is to confer with them and persuade them to cancel the engagement and so release me."

On Thursday morning after this interview I was writing at my table before a window overlooking the street when I saw a man with a large bag at his back. From it he withdrew papers and placed them under the front doors of the houses along the street. He stopped at every house. I thought nothing of it, however, until I went downstairs to dinner. Then, seeing a paper on the mat, I picked it up and glanced at it. It took but a glance to reveal its character—one of the most sensational and impure of all sheets, carrying its nature stamped on the first page in the large picture that disgraced it.

With the paper in my hand I went to the dining room and said to my host, "You have all agreed that your town is especially free from the curse of impurity, but see, the unclean demon, presuming upon your indifference or ignorance as a people, has dared perpetrate the boldest thing I ever saw attempted. Here is this paper, circulated in daylight, in all the homes, for I saw the fellow. He stopped at every door."

"That?" Coming to my side, she took the sheet from my hand. "Why, I did not know there was anything bad about that; it comes often. Of course, we never read such trashy stuff, but I thought it was only trash."

"Then look at it again—at this, and this! How could a woman's eyes fail to see such things?"

"I see now, truly; but I never thought before."

Her cheeks flushed at the sudden revelation that an intelligent glance at the unclean creature in her hand had given her, and without further ado, she opened the door of the stove and thrust it in.

In the afternoon at the institute the subject before us was the Educational Department, and the question of literature, good and bad, was brought into prominence. Allusion was made to the noontime event. As soon as the truth was out and fairly comprehended by the ladies present, one woman with an intense expression arose and asked to be excused. She explained, saying, "That same thing came to my house. I picked it up, saw the pictures, and thought they would amuse the children. So I put it on the table with the *Youth's Companion* and *St. Nicholas.* I have four boys. I want to get home quickly."

There followed upon this an awakening that shook the old town, and at the lecture on the tabooed subject the next Sabbath, the house was packed; the solemnity of eternity was upon us.

A few days after a lecture in another place, in which I had spoken of the dangers to children from impure literature, a woman called at the place where I was staying and asked to see me. She was admitted and proceeded to tell me that she went home from that lecture very angry, indignant, because the things said had compelled her to anxiety about her own boy, her only child.

She said, "It seemed disloyal to my boy to think the things you put into my mind. I kept fighting them, saying to myself, *It can't be; he has* never *seen any such vile stuff and never will.* But the more she contended against the suggestion that he might be in danger, the more troubled she became and the more incensed against the lecture and the lecturer. At last she thought, *Just to settle it and rid myself of all this anxiety, I will search his belongings. Then I can say that all about* my *boy, at least, is pure.*

She felt like a culprit as she went to his room and began the investigation, but she determined to make it thorough, that this might be the end.

"And," she said, drawing her hand from behind her back where it had been hidden, "at last, I looked all through his bed. Inside the mattress, where it had been ripped a little, I found *this.*"

It was a small paper-covered book, and as it fell open in her hand, it revealed the utmost pollution that could be placed in a picture. There was no need to inspect it closely. The mother bowed her head upon her hand and wept aloud, crying with every sobbing breath, "What shall I do? My boy! My boy!"

"Tell me about your boy," I said at length. "Tell me how he looks, how he acts at home."

"Oh," she said, "anybody would say he was a nice boy. He has a sweet face; large, dark eyes; with long, curling lashes, beautiful eyes—too beautiful ever to have looked on this—and he is always nice to me. A lovely son he has always been."

"How old is he?"

"Almost 16."

"Have you ever talked with him about himself, and his relation to your sex?"

"Never! And I resented with all my soul the counsel
you gave us mothers in your lecture. I wished you had
never come to our town. But now, if you know what a
poor mother is to do in such a case, tell me, and I'll do it."

"Of course," I said, "it would take divine wisdom to
give unerring counsel. You must have that. But to the best
of my knowledge of such a case, I should advise that you
take this book and call your boy to meet you in his own
room. Then tell him all you have felt and thought, all that
this thing is to you. Have him meet that dreadful picture
in your own presence. Tell him the true history of his
own life, how he came to be; what God means in His
Word; what such a thing as this means to his own manhood, to his own home, wife, and children. You must not
ignore the fact that manhood means fatherhood, and that
it is for you to teach your son of the sacred office and its
responsibilities, and that youth is the time for preparation
for it. That all culture, all grace, all skill, all power, are to
be subservient to fatherhood in man, and motherhood in
woman. Spare yourself nothing. Confess to him the failure
of your silence up to this point. Better tell him too much
now than not enough. Leave him nothing to surmise, to
question of anyone."

"Will you pray for me? Oh, how I shall need it!"

"Indeed I will; your cause is mine now." We prayed
together, and she went out to the hard work that lay
before her.

The day following the next she returned, and as I met
her all the questions in my mind as to results were answered. Her face was radiant with peaceful joy. There was
strength in her tone and firmness in the clasp of her hand
upon mine.

"Tell me about it," I said.

"Oh, I cannot find words!" she said. "I did it just as

you told me; and it is all right. My boy is mine as never before; we understand each other now. But oh! I tremble when I think of what would certainly have been if my eyes had not been opened."

In another home there was a bright boy of 10, proud of his strong resemblance to his father, which was re-marked about by all who saw the two. The father was a businessman; he had the habit of looking over the morning paper at breakfast and leaving for his office while the family yet lingered at the table. The boy invariably took up the paper his father had laid down and, striking the very attitude of the man, went on perusing it as he sipped his cup of strong coffee and broke his roll.

One morning as we all smiled again at the miniature man a young aunt went behind him and looked over his shoulder. With a laugh she cried out, "Oh, for pity's sake, Chat! What do you find *there* to interest you?"

"Oh, lots! It's fun!" was the reply.

"What is it, Belle? What is he reading?" asked the mother.

"Why, the *divorces!*"

"Charles!" cried the mother in disgust. "The idea! I shall tell your father to keep the paper out of the house, or take it off to the city with him."

"Guess I can find 'nother, 'f you do!" was the reply.

In yet another home, I have seen a wise father who had solved the problem of how to use the daily newspaper in his home and yet bring up his boy in purity in spite of its columns of criminality and its advertisements that were sometimes so attractive because the thing they advertised was so veiled in mystery. This was his plan: However weary he might be after the 6:00 dinner, the paper was taken from its place on the hall table, and Willie, sometimes astride the arm of his father's chair, always as near him as possible, unfolded the sheet, read the headings, and selected whatever he chose to read aloud. If the paper contained anything that promised to be especially objectionable, the father called attention to this and the boy read it, the father making his own commentary on the text, thus keeping the inside track of the evil.

The threshold of the home should be as an observatory from which, through the telescope of periodical literature, with the parent for instructor, the child should learn to view the world as it is, and properly estimate it. Some parents make the mistake of trying to keep from their children all knowledge of the evil that is in the world, but this cannot be done. Sooner or later the ever-present evil will intrude upon sight and hearing and attack the hidden senses of the soul and spirit. Children have been given these early, quiet years in the home, under parental tutorage, for the purpose of preparing them to discriminate against the impure and untrue, and to banish them from their own nature. Ignorance is never safety. Innocence is not purity. Purity is what remains after an intelligent choice of the right has been made instead of the wrong; after temptation has been met and overcome. To learn to estimate the unclean according to its nature, to think about it purely, and be able to plan for its overthrow is to come up to God's standard of purity for man and woman.

The man or woman who is ashamed of any function of the human body, who would feel disgraced to be compelled to answer the natural questions of a child concerning these, has yet to learn what purity really means. And this is the great need of motherhood and childhood today.

Unclean literature is slipped into the hand of the little girl or boy on the street, sent through the post office to the young miss or lad away at school, thrown into the front doors of the best of homes. The park and schoolyard

fences, walls of public buildings, sidewalks, school rest-
rooms, are often so disfigured by the hieroglyphics of sin
that there is no safety for the wide-awake, inquisitive child
save in *knowledge*—that knowledge of the evil that shall
make him or her afraid of it. It is true that knowledge may
be perverted to unholy use, but it is only through a proper
application of well-digested truth that the race can be
saved from the consequences of ignorance.

The children who have been banished from parlor and
family room to the little world of their own, with other
children or their own thoughts or some vile book for companions, while Mother nursed the nervousness that
should never have existed, and Daddy planned for an increase in power of some sort, or while guests were being
entertained—such deserted little ones are continual reen-
forcements to the wasting, decaying armies of vice. When
it is 20 years too late there comes the terrible awakening
to the church, to the home, that another, and another, has
so mysteriously gone astray. And the question is asked,
"How could it be, when they had such good parents?"

An old man of my acquaintance was very much concerned over the fact that his son, a promising young
lawyer, was growing more and more irreligious and indif-
ferent to those things that make good character and repu-
tation. He became so deeply alarmed that at length he
began most assiduously to press upon him the question of
personal salvation. I had known the family and was supposed to have great influence over the young man, so the
father arranged that I should be called for evangelistic
work to the town in which they resided, hoping that this
might be the means of reaching his son.

The young man understood the plan at once and, call-
ing upon me, said: "I see it is expected that I am to be
converted. My father expects it, and you are willing to

labor for it. It is only fair that you should understand how the land lies. I would like to have it settled. I have the same thing to say to you and to him, so I would like you to give us an interview. Come over to our house to dinner, and I will explain."

I went, and after dinner the young man said, "Father, I have something I want to say to you and Mrs. Henry, together. Let us go into the living room."

When we were seated he said, "There is but one course for me. I have tried not to bring on the crisis in a matter that must cause my father great sorrow, but I have concluded that now the best way is to face the facts, once for all, and have it over. Father, I shall never become a Christian. I shall try to be as good a son to you in your old age as possible, but I must be an eternal disappointment to you, because I am to myself. I believe all you have taught me. I am not in any sense of the word a skeptic. I believe that only the pure in heart can ever see God, and I never can be pure in heart."

"My son! My son!" cried the father, in a tone of agony.

"Do not interrupt me, Father," answered the young man, with pain expressed in every feature and tone. "Hear me out, please, and then for God's sake let the matter drop. I have longed a thousand times to tell you what, if it had been told when I was younger, there might have been help for. But you know, Father, we never talked. I had no one to talk to who would help me. It came about this way: When I was a little boy in school, another boy handed me a vile book to read. I was so bewilderingly terrified by its contents that to this day the impression remains. I at once hated that boy, and I hate him as a man—hate him more because, somehow, he was converted and is a preacher now.

"That was the beginning. An awful fascination took

possession of me. I have stood by my mother, and felt pale with the intense desire I had to tell her, as the months passed, and have her help me out of the horror that held me night and day. She was a good woman, but she made a great mistake with me. I never once really tried to open my heart to you, Father, but I used to wonder what fathers were for, if boys couldn't have their help. I know I am hurting you, Father, but I can't help it; it is for this once only.

"Well, that first bewildering book with its pictures was like the first glass of intoxicating liquor, only it was not watered or sugared. It was rank, bitter poison at first, and I had to know what was back of it; what it meant. The same boy kept me supplied with more of the same sort, until I learned how to get the stuff for myself, and all through my school life, my college course, and until now, my life has been feeding upon this. I hate it, but it holds me. I need not give you in detail its effects upon my career. Only this will I say: I shall never amount to anything in my profession. I have no mental grip. I have the power to see what I might have been; I have the faith to understand what I am, and shall be. I am a corrupt sinner, lost before my time, and all because of the vile things I have read and the vile life I live. You will be yet more shocked when I tell you that I have now even lost all desire to make a change, or to conceal what I am. I thought, however, I would not let you two, who care honestly for my soul, go on and work yourselves to death to try to convert me. I would tell you, once for all, just how hopeless it is. So that is all."

He took up his hat and abruptly left us. The agony of that father and my own heartache cannot be pictured. Of course we knew that if the young man could but be aroused to make an effort, if he would but truly accept

Christ, all would be changed. But the way seemed deliberately closed between him and all influence, all help, by his own hand. As yet, it cannot be opened.

I have reason to believe that many young men and young women who are burdening the heart of the church would, if they should truly answer as to why they do not come to Christ, have the same story to tell.

One such son of the church said to me, "The words of the Bible, the promises of God, have been all so mixed up with the vile things I have read and seen and done that they can never help me. They all have associations so unclean that now that I would like to be better, I cannot." But this young man learned later that the Word of God is very pure, and came to the demonstration of the fact that it can cleanse the heart and conscience of evil thought and desire.

The printed page may be a small thing, but it carries a potency too mighty to be thrust into the life of a child without the utmost care on the part of parents and friends.

Chapter 8

ANIMAL life, and the treatment it receives at the hands of "grown-up people," tell mightily upon the character of the child. God should be so recognized in all His works that life, wherever found, should be held sacred.

To teach a child to kill even a fly wantonly is to destroy some fine quality of the soul that the child cannot afford to lose. And yet in how few homes is any thought given to this subject. How many fathers and mothers will even laugh to ridicule the teaching of this page as they read it. Someone will say, "But shall flies and bugs and worms and spiders be allowed to overrun us?"

There is reason to protect ourselves from the inroads of vermin. When this cannot be done by natural means, the unnatural must sometimes be resorted to. But *killing* by the human is *always* unnatural. The effect of the slaughterhouse upon the character of man is an illustration of the result of even the most respectable and useful sort of killing.

A businessman of wide observation once said to me, "If I wanted to give a boy a shortcut to perdition, I would either set him to raising animals to kill or to killing them for market." It is nothing unusual to see children and adults catching fish for no reason but "for fun." Shooting simply for the sport is but a milder manifestation of the same spirit that instigated the gladiatorial exhibitions of Rome and the bullfights of Spain.

The letting out of blood is something that is not easily stayed; and the child who stands by, watching, with curious, painful pleasure, as you crush a bug that might just as well have been placed outside the screen into the open air where there is room enough for its little life; the boy who gloats over the death agonies of the chicken being prepared for supper, will not have to go much farther on the same road to be able to take human life.

The murderous spirit of this age may be traced directly back to the demoralizing sports of the chase, in the great preserves of the motherlands across the sea. It has been inflamed by the passions and poisons that, like fires that never cool, have preserved the evil inheritance through the generations.

Arbitrary decisions and commands that leave no room for the operation of the free will of the child work evils that are so grave that they deserve more than a passing notice. It is our business to make character in our children. But character cannot develop except by liberty of thought and choice. Too often children are expected to be Christians simply because their fathers and mothers are. In one sense this is right, because the promise is "unto us and to our children"; but if the child becomes a church member—a "professor"—simply because he was brought up that way, he lacks that which is necessary to a true Christian experience. Just as soon as he begins to question, as he must question if he ever knows the truth for himself, he is often impeached as an unbeliever.

A dinner party of Christian workers was gathered in the home of a minister. The after-dinner conversation drifted into discussion of a certain preacher who had been suspected of too liberal views. Opinions were freely exchanged, and while the spirit of the conversation was most genial and kindly, just the sort to draw out latent questionings, there sat in a corner, quietly but eagerly listening, the son of the host, a youth of about 19. As there was a little lull in the general flow of ideas, he ventured to remark that he wished he knew how anyone could be as positive about the inspiration of the Bible as about the facts of history.

Instantly many kind, sympathetic faces turned toward the boy; many hearts went out to him. But his father, with a heavy frown and a look of deep annoyance, swept the circle with a deprecating apologetic glance and then said to his son in a stern, indignant tone, "Such a question as *that* from a boy that has been brought up as you have!"

The young fellow's eyes dropped. He was mortified and resentful. An embarrassed pause, followed by the murmur of many voices as the guests tried to hide the confusion of the moment, ensued, under cover of which the young man arose and left the room with a look on his face that I would not like to see on the face of my boy.

His question was not unusual. Probably every minister in that company, every Christian of any positiveness of character, had at some time had the same thought, and had because of it been driven nearer to the Source of truth and into deeper Christian experience. Among the number were many who should have been able to take the thought of that boy in tow and lead him out into the clear depths of true and sure seeking after God. But as the case was left, the sad question would come, "Who shall help him? To whom shall the boy go for answers, when his father, a teacher in the Lord's house, repudiates his right to ask for himself?"

In a family of children in this day, when the world encroaches so closely upon the church, there is continual necessity of intelligent and correct choice between the things that are right and those that are wrong. When selection is always made by the parent, and the child can but accept an arbitrary decision and be governed by it, there is imminent danger. By and by, when the changes that often come so suddenly leave the young man or woman alone, he or she is like the lame from whom the crutch has been taken; like a ship without a rudder, drifting with the tide, ready to be led anywhere by any pirate craft that comes over the high seas.

A mother with three boys and a girl to rear alone learned the grace of liberality toward her children. She did not try to make all their decisions for them. She would take time to present the why and whither of each question that came from the children to her, and then leave them to make their own free choice.

When asked if she was not afraid they would sometimes make a disastrous choice she replied, "That is just why I adopted this method. How should they ever be able to choose wisely if they do not practice? If my sons and daughter are ever going to make a dangerous choice of the ways that promise success and happiness, I want them to do it while they are young enough to yet have time to learn how to live, and while they have mother and home to help them repair the mischief."

One evening her eldest son, a boy of 13, came in with the announcement that he had been invited to a children's party. He asked if he might go, adding that he was expected to take some girl with him. He had never before been brought to the necessity of a choice on this point. Their lives had been so quiet and simple that juvenile "society" had taken no note of them, and there had been nothing to call forth special teaching from the mother. The opening of the subject was, therefore, a surprise and also an annoyance, because her ideas were at variance on the subject with those of average mothers.

She did not believe in children's evening parties. She believed in nothing, from a church festival and concert down, that would transform a 13-year-old boy into a beau or cause a young girl to expect him as her escort. But she knew that it would be very unwise to say this to her spirited, dark-eyed boy. So, positively resisting the indignant impulses that were astir within her, she said, "We will talk this over before bedtime."

When the time came, and the children all gathered for their "before-bedtime talk," the matter of the party was taken up and discussed, not controversially but in quiet, candid fashion. The mother gave the children the "first say," according to custom, and then in her plain way, which left nothing for surmise or speculation, she gave them a view of both sides of the question, bringing, as nearly as possible, the lens of her own experience to the eyes of her children. When she had gone over the ground, she said, "Now, my son, you understand this matter as well as I do. You must do as you choose about going. If you decide to go, I will get you ready as nicely as I can afford."

"But Mama," cried the boy in a tone of perplexity, "I don't want it left that way this time. There's too much in it."

"But it is for you, and you alone, to decide."

"Well, then, please tell me what you would do if you were a boy like me."

That mother has often said that nothing had ever so thrilled her as this putting of the question by her boy. She thanked God in her heart that she had been able to keep her life near enough to his that he could even imagine her being a boy like him.

As she waited an instant, the other children took up the plea for a decision from her. "Yes, Mama, tell us what you would do if you were a little boy."

"Very well," she said, "I will tell you as nearly as I can. If I could step over all the barriers of years and sex, and be a boy like you, Willie, and still take my experience of life with me; if I could know what I know today and yet be a boy like you, I should send polite 'regrets' in answer to the kindly intended invitation, and then go right on in my own natural, healthful life. On that evening I should have my 'before-bedtime talk' as usual; go to bed at 9:00 as usual; and, as usual, sleep all night and be rested and fresh the next morning. I would go to school on time, thoroughly prepared, and keep my own place in my class, while those who went to the party would come with headaches, be cross and nervous, find fault and be found fault with, and fail in lessons. I would save myself the pleasures of an evening's social gathering until I was really ready to enjoy such things, just as I would the satisfaction of business and homemaking, until I had been prepared for them. You can do as you choose, but this is what *I* would do if I could be a boy and yet know what I know now."

Willie drew a long, deep breath, and said, "And that's just what I'll do, Mama. But," he added earnestly after a moment, "you might just as well have told me in the first place that I couldn't go!"

"Certainly not, my son; for you can go if you choose; there is nothing to hinder. I told you I would help you off, and I will."

"But, of course, after what you have told me, I don't want to go."

"Then you are the one that says you can't go, not I."

"Who'd want to go after what you said?"

"You believe I said the truth?"

"Of course; but I did want to go so much."

"Yes? Why not now, then?"

"Because—because—of what you said."

"If you did not believe I told the truth, what then?"

"Why, of course—but I couldn't believe that."

"And so by what I said, you know more than you did

before supper?"

"Yes."

"Well, then, you see it was much better that we talked it over than that I should have forbidden your going and not taught you the truth. Now you are just as independent about it as I am, because you *know* things. I think that is the grand thing about *knowing,* for it helps you decide."

"So do I, and if things are *so* about things, of course a fellow wants to know it; but I don't see why it's *got* to be so, and spoil a fellow's fun."

"It is the wrong and unnatural things that spoil our fun. We must accept things as they are and take the consequences. It is with these social questions just as with eating and drinking. If you take things into your stomach that do not agree with you, no matter how well you like their taste, you have to repent with pain, and it is not the part of an intelligent being to do that, is it?"

"Of course not. It's all right, Mama. I don't want to spoil myself with anything, and I am ever so glad you don't let me go on without telling me things."

I have given this talk because it opens up, through this boy's reception of the truth, a solution of the great problem of the preservation of our children from ruin.

If "my people are destroyed for lack of knowledge," they are to be saved only by the word of truth. "Now ye are clean through the word which I have spoken unto you."

Children are too often left to experiment with evil and to find out, by baleful results to themselves, that it would have been better to have denied curiosity and put a thousand leagues between the attractive seducer and self-indulgence. Even in Christian homes they are sometimes led into the first steps downward.

"You can't keep a child in a straitjacket—he must know for himself: hence, let him play cards, let him drink moderately, if he wants to; let him sow his wild oats; let him go anywhere, everywhere, and find out the world for himself" is the teaching.

"Of course," said a Christian mother, "I would not play cards, or dance, or go to the theater, for I am a Christian. But my children do not profess anything of the sort, and you can't hold them to a straitlaced mode of life." And so her children went into all worldliness.

"My boys will play cards, and smoke, and drink beer," said another; "and if they will do it, they shall do it at home." And so that home presented the appearance and had the odors of a third-rate boardinghouse, while every sense that belonged to a refined Christian woman was blunted, or destroyed, in the mother.

What is right for one person under the same gospel dispensation is right for another—for everyone. God has given one rule for all to live and work by. He has issued no indulgences, no licenses. He excuses no child or man or woman from the obligations of careful, pure, useful living simply because they "do not profess to be good." Anything in social or personal indulgence that is safe for one is safe for another, under the same conditions. Poisons such as alcohol, nicotine, and other drugs have their one way with all animal tissue, and beget the same demoralized appetites. They do precisely the same deadly work whether used in a Christian home or in a bar. Gambling and games of chance, wherever played, work the same pernicious influence in cultivating the qualities of mind and heart that are nurtured at the peril of virtue.

The modern dance, whether in living room or hall, tends to the same impurities in thought and life.

The only method of really protecting our children from the results of these evil things is by teaching them carefully, plainly, all truth involved in them. We must always "take the chance" of their reception or rejection of the truth after they come to know it. It is inconsistent with the profession of Christ to do any forbidden thing. Yet Christianity is not an arbitrary system of unreasonable requirements, as it is too often regarded, even by the children of the church. It is but a benevolent device for the most kindly protection of us all from the things that are deadly to all happiness.

The power to command the confidence of the child, so that like Willie he will accept parental instruction as the end of controversy, is the output of truth in the inward parts.

In many professedly Christian homes there is a woeful lack of this necessary constituent of success in child rearing. Children are even lied to, in places where a lie is not to be expected. Prevarication is resorted to, to meet the embarrassing question.

When the child wants to know, as is his right, concerning his own origin or from whence his beloved baby sister came, he is told that the doctor or nurse brought her, or given a yet more obscure reply. These lies satisfy the poor little innocent until he learns better.

A mother and child were on a railroad train. The child was full of questions and restless. The mother tried to keep him quiet while she read to herself. The train stopped at a station and the child fretted to get off. At last the mother, seizing him, said roughly, "If you don't stop your noise, I'll open the window and throw you out!"

The little fellow gave her a startled look, then with a smile that said, *Oh, I know what that means,* settled for a moment quietly against her. But only for a moment; he was tired, and again he began fretting.

"Now, see here," demanded the mother. "Look out there! Do you see that man with the blue coat? He's a brakeman; that means that he breaks up little boys that fuss as you do. He'll come in in a minute, and I'll give you to him. If you don't mind me he'll break you."

The train began to move, and the brakeman swung himself aboard and came into the car. The child rolled his eyes toward him. Somebody said, "Brakeman," and he paused near the seat occupied by the mother and child.

"There! He's going to take you; he shall have you," she began, while the absolute terror of the little one was pitiful to see. But the man passed on, the child watching him until he evidently remembered other unfulfilled threats that had been hurled at him. Turning, he spat into his mother's face with an expression of repudiation that cannot be pictured. She laughed angrily, sarcastically, at him, and held his hands as he tried to strike her. Many who looked on helplessly were asking themselves, *What is the future of that child, with such a guide of his youth?*

A WCTU lecturer was taken home one evening by a member of the temperance union; the host was accompanied by an interesting boy of about 4 years. The child was very tired and sleepy, and demanded immediate attention. But the mother was eager to make her guest comfortable after a fatiguing journey and the labor of the evening, so she put the little one off. He kept following her about, plucking at her dress and whining. At length the mother paused, took him by the shoulders, turned him about, and said, "Do you see Mrs. ———? What do you suppose she thinks of you? She has some little boys, and they never acted like this."

The visitor wanted to quiet the youngster with a story, but she was too weary to come up with one.

Her host went on about her preparations. The child stood and looked at the guest a moment with curious interest, then, whining, turned to his mother. She allowed him to tease but a moment when, taking him by the shoulder again, she said:

"Now, look at Mrs. ———! She doesn't like little boys that act so. She wants me to get her lunch. She's tired, and you must keep still. If you don't, I'll hand you over to her, and she'll throw you into the garbage."

The little fellow glared up at their guest as if she were a human monster, and he had a perfect right to think so.

The motherly, truehearted visitor could not endure the torture of his fearful gaze, and so she answered on his behalf and that of truth: "My dear woman, you belong to our temperance movement; you are one of us, so I must be allowed to speak, now. What are you teaching that child? If you believed that I was capable of doing what you have said, you would not have allowed me in your house. I never threw a child into the garbage in my life, and I never shall. If, by any chance, it were necessary for you to give your boy to me, you know I would not, could not, do this dreadful thing. What will he think of the cause I represent as he grows up, if you teach him this and he believes you?"

Incidents might be multiplied ad infinitum in which falsehood has been resorted to as a means of discipline, and we are reaping the result in the young all about us.

All parents stand as the representatives of God to their little children; and when the knowledge of the facts comes to children, along with evidence that they have not been told the truth or fairly dealt with; when they come to know better than to believe all the silly things they have been told, they have also gained the loss of all things that should be in the foundation of character, and which nothing can restore. To find the word of father or mother unreliable is to begin to doubt all truth. By this process, many a child has been developed into an infidel. Many a one has been lost to truth and Christ after learning that the parents, whom they should reverence above all but God, were less than they had supposed them to be. I doubt if a child ever recovers from the shock of the discovery that he has not been candidly dealt with by his parents.

This candor covers more ground than appears at sight. The child has rights of many sorts, which adults are bound to respect. Not only do children's rights cover the ground of their personal possessions, and the most faithful teaching concerning the things that are needful for them to know, but they have a right to the best things in the personal experience of their parents: the sacred things of love, and faith, and hope—and rectified failure, and forgiven wrong. They have a right to know the peculiar things of physical or mental inheritance that should be suppressed, as well as those that should be cultivated. If something sweet, poetic, something from God, comes to the parent, it should be shared with the child. They have a right to a frank confession from their parents if they have done wrong by the child. Parents who will not acknowledge a wrong to their children need never expect frankness in return for duplicity.

A WCTU worker gives two incidents that illustrate what I wish to convey. A pastor came to her, saying, "Can you help us about my son? He has not been home for three days and nights, and his mother is almost wild with worry and concern."

"I will do all I can for you," she replied.

"Well, first, he must be found. I am afraid he is in one of the dens of vice of this city. I wish you would find him and get him out."

"Find him! Surely you know that I could do nothing for him in that way. If I were to find him, as you say, and attempt to get him out, I would bring upon him the ridicule of all his companions and make it impossible that I could ever speak to him. Of course he must be found and taken out, taken home, but not by me."

"Well, then, I will get the police to find him and bring him home, and then when he gets sobered up we will invite you over and manage it so that you will be left alone with him. Then you can give him a good talking-to, and make him see just where he stands."

"Neither will that do," she replied. "Your son knows about my work; he knows that I never go anywhere by accident. He would see at once that it was a trap. Boys don't like traps; neither do I. I never deal in them. I will tell you what you'd better do. Get him home the best way you can. Get him sober, then have a talk with him and persuade him to come down here, if you think I can help him, and I will be glad to talk with him. Get him to take a step toward this himself. Then I can say to him whatever seems best."

"Ah, but he would never come here. I do believe you could help him if you would but take the trouble to come to our house."

"Certainly I would count nothing trouble. Let him know that I am coming, get his consent to see me, and I will go gladly."

"He wouldn't consent to see you," said the father impatiently. "He would get out of the way, unless you should get him where he would either have to be rude to you or listen. He would not be rude, so you would have your chance."

"I could never take such a chance as that, simply because I could do no good but would surely do harm. The only way that I can see to be practical is for you to talk to him. Get him home, give him time to become sober. Then, after he has retired for the night, go to his room; get as close to him as you can, and tell him all the deep, tender things that are in your heart—all your fear, your love, your desire before God for his soul. Let him into it all if possible; and then, when you have done all you can, you can commend him to God. I will gladly do anything right, but I really believe this is the only way."

The father had risen, and as she concluded he turned his face to the wall and stood struggling with emotion. At length he turned about and with the tears on his cheeks said, "Mrs. ———, I have a shameful confession to make. I have never in my life talked to my boy about the salvation of his soul, or any of these things, and I can't begin now. If he is ever saved, it must be through somebody besides me."

"Then, sir," she said, her voice trembling in its indignation, "if you have done this—allowed your own son to grow up to be 22 years old, and have never, as you say, talked to him about these things, *you* have the work to do; and God will hold you responsible. Find him, if you have to get the police to help. Get him home, as I said. When you go to his room, don't turn on the light—you could not endure the light—but get down on your knees by his bed and tell him that you are the one that is to blame; that you are the one to be punished, because you never have taught him what he had to know for salvation. Ask him to forgive you; tell him how you love him; how your heart is breaking. Cast yourself and your interest in his soul upon his mercy—his chivalry, as a young man, toward your gray hairs and his mother's sorrow. Promise to stand by him in all the fight for his lost manhood, and then leave the rest to him and God. I see no other way for you."

He stood trembling and white.

"It ought to be done," he said, "but it will be very hard."

"Of course—nothing can be easy in a case like this."

He went away, bowed under the terrible burden. Whatever resulted is not known, only that the young man still went on in the downward path, and that the father ever after avoided that worker.

The other incident related by the same woman is identical in many points but has important differences. The father was a businessman, and he was surprised out of his absorption in his work by the discovery that his son was already far gone in the way to ruin, in spite of all that his Christian home had been to him.

The father came to the worker for help in his trouble, and when she discovered that he had made the same failure as the minister, she gave him the same solution of the difficulty. After a notable struggle with his pride, he said, "I will do it, God helping me! Will you pray for me?"

"Indeed I will," she said. "If you find him today, it will probably be about 10:00 tonight when you will get around to have your talk with him. I will pray for you and him at 10:00."

What resulted is known only by a few things that came before the public. When next that young man was seen upon the street, he was in company with his father, not as a culprit who must be watched and kept in tow, but as a companion. And from that time, when you saw one, as a rule you saw the other. After a while the son was given a position of trust, and later, as a Christian, was associated with his father in the church and its work.

One very important thing needed by the children of the church today is more real *fatherhood* in the home and in government, and a more enlightened motherhood; consecrated, enlightened, honest parentage is the need of the nation.

We have before us the task of making possible a race that shall receive Christ as king, and bring in the day when His Word shall be the end of controversy. There is no need that one son or daughter of our prayers shall fail to take a true man's, a pure woman's, part in the blessed evolution of all things good, out of the beginnings in the hands of the church and nation.

Ruin is not their inheritance, under God. Sorrow and disappointment have not been appointed for our portion as parents. God intended that every one of us should be the spiritual parents of our own children, leading them all the way from birth to regeneration, and not one word of His promise shall fail.

According to our faith (obedience) shall it be with us. If we work and pray and believe for salvation, we shall have it. But if our works are disobedience and faithlessness, we shall have desolation and sorrow in our homes, as a nation, and as a church.

Mothers must not flinch from the task before them, and fathers must learn that paternal care that will cause them to leave every evil habit and association for the child's sake.

"Our Father which art in heaven" must find embodiment in the flesh, in our homes. The motherhood of God must be expressed before our children, in government and law. Then shall the day come when the righteous nation, born and bred of us, shall "go through the gates" and take possession of the peaceful inheritance of the children of God.

Chapter 9

HAT is prayer, and what are the conditions upon which its answer is based?" is a question of special importance in the relation between the parent and child.

Prayer is just as reasonable and natural as is ordinary conversation in the home, and will get just as satisfactory replies as a good, careful mother will give her little one.

It is *asking,* not *addressing,* the Almighty.

Before we can really ask for anything we must want it, must know we need it, and must know that we have come to the proper place at which to ask. If we want bread, we never think of stopping at a hardware store for it. If we want the things of sensuality, of indulgence, we cannot with any sincerity ask God for them, for we know He does not deal in such things. If we want and feel that we need the things that make for purity, truth, good character—anything that the world is unable to give us—we come to God for them. It is for the time of need that God has provided.

"Blessed are they which do hunger and thirst after righteousness: for they shall be filled." "Come boldly unto the throne of grace, that we may obtain mercy, and find grace to help in time of need." "My God shall supply all your need." "I came not to call the righteous, but sinners." "They that are *whole* have no need of the physician, but they that are sick." These and kindred passages plainly teach us that He has made provision for a time of necessity.

And the need must be *personal.* We never make an effort to get anything for which we have no personal need. We may be of generous spirit, and desire to take all blessing to the needy about us, but only as we feel personally for them are we moved to effort in their behalf. The unfeeling heart goes on, regardless of others' woes. Christ, *"touched with the feeling* of our infirmities," was able to work out deliverance for us. The woman who brought her daughter to Jesus cried out, "Lord, help *me!"* If the daughter was not healed, *she,* the mother, was not herself helped, and this personality of need gave effectiveness to her asking.

Anything that we absolutely need we make every effort to obtain. We try our own resources, and come to the end of them; then we reach out to those nearest us, and on out to everything that promises a supply, until we have gone to the limit of things seen and known. Then and not until then can we ask of God. God has made no provision to do for us anything that we can do for ourselves, or that we can with propriety get others to do for us.

David cried out, "Unless the Lord had been my help, my soul had almost dwelt in silence." "Give us help from trouble: for vain is the help of man." But he had to learn these things by his own failure to do for himself, or to get from the powers of this world that which would satisfy his need.

So with us. We cannot save our children or ourselves, but before we can with truth pray for their salvation, their preservation from the snares of ruin, we must do all in our power for their salvation. We must make our lives right by God's grace; we must make all the conditions about the child in the home as nearly right as possible; we must keep out of the home everything that tends to demoralize; must banish from the kitchen and the dining table everything that will awaken or create depraved appetite; must expel from the living room, the family room, anything that cannot be used to build up pure thought and soundness of purpose; and we must bring around our children, according to our ability, everything that will aid in the work of salvation.

We must do all in our power to cleanse the streets that they must tread, the store windows, the bookstalls, of impurity; we must see that, so far as we can do it, the laws are made right. Then, when we have done all we can and sent out our influence as widely as possible to this end, we are in condition truly to ask God to finish the work and to bring to pass the desire of our heart that prompted all these efforts on our part.

We must learn what we can do by actual effort. We must learn what we can get done by the same means. Then we shall know what remains for God to do. When we come to the end of our resources, we are just at the place where God's abundance begins, and not before.

Then we must hold in honor the simple means that God has ordained—the small things that are within the reach of small human strength. "Ask, and it shall be given you; seek, and ye shall find; knock, and it shall be opened unto you." "Therefore I say unto you, What things soever ye desire, when ye pray, believe that ye receive them, and ye shall have them."

"What doth it profit, my brethren, though a man say he hath faith, and have not works? can faith save him? If a brother or sister be naked, and destitute of daily food, and one of you say unto them, Depart in peace, be ye warmed and filled; notwithstanding ye give them not those things which are needful to the body; what doth it profit?"

Even so, if we pray for our children and yet despise the simple, homely means of honesty, loving-kindness, benevolence, family, as well as business, religion, and political Christianity, all our faith, so-called, will not save them through us.

The ordinary things of human life are, in our hands, God's most effective means for their salvation. I know a bright boy whom I dearly loved, who, as he grew, began to go in wrong ways. I met him one day after he had just come out of a bar and I said, "Willie, I wish you would not go into bars."

"Why not?" he answered, with quick heat.

"Because they are bad, wholly bad."

"I don't think so," he interrupted. "If they were, my father would not vote for them, for he is a good man."

What more could I say? His father was a good man, but he lived to see that mere goodness would not save him from the sorrow of ruin in his son. He had despised the ballot as a means of salvation; had construed its mission from a purely business and political standpoint, and so suffered, and still suffers today. One man complained to me that he had not a lively faith, and was therefore crippled as a Christian. So it would be. But a lively faith depends upon lively obedience. The sum of our ability to believe and trust God is always equal to the measure of our actual obedience.

"To obey is better than sacrifice." Dogged obedience, an awkward, blundering obedience, is better than any amount of sentimental faith. "Whatsoever we ask, we receive of him, because we keep his commandments, and do those things that are pleasing in his sight."

To do the right things, we must know what they are. "Be ye not unwise, but understanding what the will of the Lord is." This refers us back to the Word of God, "Search the Scriptures." Familiarity with the Word and will of God is of absolute importance if we are going to pray; for God will not give us things that, under the same conditions, He would have denied to anybody else. Nor will He grant us anything that is contrary to His will; so we must know what His will is.

I have seen Christian parents who were afraid of God's will. They could not say "The will of the Lord be done" without a great effort.

One Christian mother, who had asked for prayer for her daughter, a beautiful girl, came to me at the close of a study on consecration and said, with deep feeling, "I feel the force of all you have said, but I do not dare say to God, 'You may take me and all I have, and do what You will with me.'"

"Why not?" I asked.

"Well, because I am afraid. You know my beautiful Cora?"

"Yes, I know Cora, and she is beautiful; but what has that to do with hindering you?"

"Oh, I am so afraid that if I should say this to God, He would take her away from me."

"How could that be?" I cried in painful surprise, and almost indignantly.

"Why, you know, He does such things."

"No, I know He does *not* do such things."

"Does not?"

"Never! Never! You need to know God better, to become acquainted with Him and His will. Suppose Cora should come to you, bringing all the beautiful things that have been given her, the choice things from abroad, and say, 'Here, Mother, take these and use them as you like; you have control of the home and can manage with them so that we shall all enjoy them better than I can,' what would you do?"

"I should be glad, for she keeps them in the cabinet in her room, and only brings them out once in a while, on special occasions."

"Yes, but what would you do with them?"

"Why, I should have her help me arrange them

tastefully for decoration, so we could all get the most out of them."

"Would you really? Would you not rather begin at once to break and destroy them in her sight?"

"Why! What a question! You know I wouldn't."

"Why not?"

"It wouldn't be *in me* to do such a thing."

"Why not?"

"Why, if for no other reason, because I'm human, and Cora *cares* for them."

"And is your heart, your humanity, so much more tender, careful, generous toward your child than your heavenly Father's nature toward His child? If you are careful of Cora's things and careful of her feelings simply because you are a human mother, how much more will God, your Father, care for your things and your feelings because He is God and you are His child. Notice how Cora's spirit toward you is the exact copy of yours toward God. You do not trust Him with your all; she keeps her choice trinkets locked up in a cabinet in her own room."

"I see."

A better acquaintance with God is a great need of the church and of the world.

The fact is that His will is the one thing to be desired. It is the only thing in the whole universe that is persistently, positively, continually seeking our well-being. Everything else is seeking to get us into trouble. It is His will having free course in us that alone can make us glad, in spite of the devices of sorrow. Before we understand this, however, we must know what it is truly to abide in Christ and have His Word abide in us. This means to have memory filled with the Word, and to have in us the mind that was in Christ; to look at things from His standpoint; to let His Word be the end of controversy. If He says a thing is wrong, to let that suffice whether it seems wrong to us or not. When He says, "This is the way," to walk in it, no matter how much we may want to go in another.

And all our praying must be in Jesus' name, not simply closing with the phrase "And all I ask is for Christ's sake and in His name," but with the spirit that recognizes God's right as did Christ.

Said a woman to me, "I came to ask you to pray for my husband," and the tears began to flow.

My heart was touched at once, and I answered, "Certainly I will, but first let us talk it over."

"There isn't much to talk about," she said, "only the fact is, if he isn't converted, so he'll stop drinking and behave, we'll just have to leave him—that's all there is about it. And then what can I do, with all the children?"

"You think, then, that if he were converted you could live with him, and keep your home, and all would go along easily."

"I do—I haven't a doubt of it. He'd be a new man, of course, and—"

"It's a new man, then, that you want."

"I think it is time I had one, don't you?"

"I do, indeed."

"Yes, and so I made up my mind I'd just come over this morning and ask you to pray that he might be converted—because I've noticed that if a man just signs the pledge of temperance but isn't converted, he doesn't stick long. If we live as a family any longer, my husband's got to leave liquor alone. I've prayed and prayed, and it doesn't do any good."

The reason of failure in a case like this could be traceable to the fact that the Lord is not a merchant, and will not be treated as one. This woman doubtless said "for Jesus' sake," but in reality her prayer was offered in the name of her own personal ease and safety. She asked God to save her husband just as she would ask to have an up-holstered chair sent her from the store, or a broken step in the stairs mended.

A minister sent for me to do evangelistic work in a fast-growing Western town. From the first there was great interest upon the part of the ungodly and drinking masses, but no power in the evangelistic crew. Everything went hard in spite of large congregations. For about 10 days we dragged along like drawing a load of stone through sand. Then, after a sleepless night and a little conversation with the pastor, I discovered that this work had been initiated with the expectation that many converts would be added to the church, and thus the salary of the pastor could be increased to a living wage. This was, of course, all right in its place, but as the motive of the effort it was on the same level as the impulses that cause two rival companies to jostle for business. Prayer and effort had been like that of which the Word of God says, "Ye ask, and receive not, because ye ask amiss, that ye may consume it upon your lusts."

For implicit directions concerning prayer, consult Matthew 6:6; Philippians 4:19; Hebrews 4:16; Psalms 94:17, 60:11; Luke 11:9, 10; Mark 11:24; 1 John 3:22; Ephesians 5:17; John 15:7, 14:14. From these teachings of the Word we learn that to pray the really effectual prayer there must be:

1. A sense of need.
2. Knowledge of our own inability.
3. Knowledge of the insufficiency of all the world as well.
4. Honor for ordained means and willingness to use them.
5. Faith and obedience.
6. Knowledge of God's will.

7. Abiding in Christ.

8. Asking in His name.

Given these conditions, there can be no possible failure.

Chapter 10

S this book may fall into the hands of some who will say, "Then everything rests with the parent," I cannot conclude without a further word:

God has made it impossible for neglect upon the part of any parent wholly to wreck the life of any child; nor shall it be possible for any child to look back from a wasted life and say to father or mother, "You have made me all I am—to you attaches the whole responsibility."

The responsibility of the parent is great, but no less is that of the individual man or woman. There comes a time when it is shifted wholly, a time when men and women are able to see and recognize under the light of God's Spirit the points of failure in their own lives and character, to repair that which has been wrongly done, and in themselves to restore the waste places, if they will accept the gospel plan.

A mother who had miserably failed awoke to see the truth when her son was a wreck at 24 years of age. She came to her son and with a brokenhearted emphasis said, "I have failed. I led you wrong, but now that you have found out how wrong it all was, don't break my heart by going on. I was careless, wicked, but I have been made sorry; and now you are a man and know just what is wrong and why. I pray you forgive me, and begin to do the right."

This shifting of the responsibilities upon her son was more than he could endure, and he did "cease to do evil" and "learn to do well."

A young man said, "I was brought up all wrong—

everything was all wrong, so there is no hope for me."

"The fact that you know that it was all wrong," was the reply, "takes the responsibility from those who brought you up and, from this day, lays it upon you. If you see the wrong, you also know the right, and if you will take God's plan and His help, nothing shall be able to destroy God's eternal hope for you. You have your own life to make. You are to become the manufacturer even of your own body, taking the things that the earth produces and, through your selection of the good or evil things you eat, make for strength or weakness. So with your thoughts. By the things you choose to look at, to hear, to touch, you control your thoughts; and your thoughts make your face, your form, your actions, your life."

The children who with filial chivalry will seek to honor their parents by making of themselves better people than the parents had reason to expect as the result of their work, will reap the fullness of the promise "Honour thy father and thy mother: that thy days may be long upon the land which the Lord thy God giveth thee."

❦ ❦ ❦

The baneful habit of selfishness grows, of necessity, in the heart of childhood, under the ordinary teaching of our day—and nothing more surely leads to the destruction of all that is noble in character. "You must learn to wait upon *yourself*" and "Attend to *your own* affairs" are mottoes inculcated from the earliest dawn of intelligence. These sound well—but anything that repeatedly calls the attention of the child to self and one's own things is to be deprecated. The scriptural injunction to "look . . . every man also on the things of others" instead of his own has divine wisdom behind it.

In one home I heard repeatedly this command or

something similar: "John, go and hang up your cap, and Charles, hang up *yours.*"

John or Charles would step over the cap of his brother to pick up his own; all personal responsibility ended when *his own* was in its proper place.

Not long ago I learned of a home in which existed a scarcely credible state of affairs, the result of the practical application of these maxims, but later I have found that it is by no means an isolated case. There were five daughters, all well grown. The family were in moderate yet comfortable circumstances. It had been a proud boast among them that each member of the household was self-reliant, doing his or her own part. The beauty of the system in which everyone attends to their own affairs, leaving others to do the same, at last developed into an astonishing domestic phenomenon. Each daughter would wash and iron her own garments and her own share of the articles for the house and the parents, but nothing besides, except in case of illness.

Each wished to get her work done as early in the day as possible, and the effort of each to have the washing done all on the same day resulted in strife and contention over the possession of the washer and room. At last the father stepped in with an arbitrary solution—he gave the girls each a day, according to her age, in which she should have undisputed control of the field! And so for five days every week the operation of washing and ironing was carried on in the little kitchen, which had to serve as laundry also. For five days consecutively, clothes were swinging from the line in the little backyard.

I have seen a better way—a home in which each did for the other, beginning as soon as the little limbs could toddle, doing absolutely *nothing simply for self.* The mother did nothing for herself that a child could do for her, and her hands were in turn always busy for them, and theirs for each other.

Did Johnny drop his cap carelessly? He was surely soon to be compelled, by the spirit of his home, to spring to pick it up before mother or sister or brother could get to it to put it in its place. Was anything left about? The first one who found it was supposed to take care of it. Under this kind of common spirit there was less carelessness among the children than in the home where "don't" and "do" constantly ring the changes on juvenile delinquency.

I believe the most effective method of making orderly, helpful, generous children in any home where mutual love is the law is for all so to share in those things that are required, that each will know that anything left lying about will cause an extra step for *someone*. I have seen a boy spring to take the hastily dropped cap, ball, or book and put it in place because he saw mother or sister about to do it for him. And he in doing this for himself had as the chief motive the desire to save them the step.

A whole household with which I am acquainted has been made careful of all personal effects by this generous system of reciprocity, and the saving in the wear and tear of tongue and temper is not the least of the benefits accruing from this plan of mutual service.

❦ ❦ ❦

Concerning crimes against the life of the unborn, I wish to add to that which appears in the body of this book. Even in professedly Christian homes is there need of the most careful and the plainest gospel teaching.

There is need of reformation in the marital relation. There must be both reformation and transformation among husbands and wives in ideas and practice, before we can have salvation as a people. Men must learn just what is the true interpretation of the scriptural injunction, "Wives, submit yourselves unto your own husbands, as unto the Lord. For the husband is the head of the wife, even as Christ is the head of the church: and he is the saviour of the body" (Eph. 5:22, 23).

The man who would father sons and daughters who shall give him honor and joy must not painfully force motherhood upon a weary, unwilling woman. But he must so reverence her person, and recognize her right to elect the time and conditions when creative powers shall be evoked, that he and she may truly claim the promise given to *those two who shall agree* in anything in *His name.* Fundamental to all causes of ruin in children are those efforts to arrest the processes of life.

The man or woman who shall, together or singly, conspire and plan to rob a human of its right to be sought after, to be made lovingly welcome, to be expected and prepared for with all sweet and tender thoughts and ministrations, shall fail in realizing the true joys of life; and shall, for every criminal thought and attempt against its life, reap thorns and thistles from the home garden, in place of the fruits of love and virtue.

In the case of the overburdened, Christless slave of a husband who will not control his passions, who in great physical weakness must bring forth children of sorrows, judgment must be tempered with tender pity even if she shall interfere to stay the little one in its passage from the "somewhere" to the "here," and at the same time provide for herself a little respite, as she hopes, from intolerable cares. But it is not for such mothers that this argument has been set forth. The *Christian* home, and the awful disaster that has overtaken it in this latter time, is the subject under consideration.

It is a fact that the church should consider that her

own work, the service of the Lord's house, has been made
the excuse for that crime against the law of God about
which tongue and pen should speak with sufficient force
and clearness to be fully understood by thousands who
need the warning most. In a certain new home we find an
illustration. Its heads were two young people of the
church—active, useful, good singers, in demand. She, especially, was a fine musician, needed at all sorts of doings,
and "so available," "having no incumbrances"; one whom
the church would miss if anything should happen to take
her out of its regular service. By and by to this pair there
came the first faint utterance of a new existence. In the secret chamber of the temple of God there was begun the
movement of that divine symphony to which the psalm of
life was to be newly sung. And while heaven's choirs
were beginning to tune their instruments and all the forces
of being waited in expectation to be called into glad service, it was found that this was not among the plans of
the young couple, or at least not at just this point in life.
Matters were getting "ahead of time," and this accidental
disarrangement, this unexpected pregnancy, was going to
interfere with their plans.

What could be done about it? The young people were
chagrined; the social and religious engagements for the
season urged *something*. There was but one of two things:
either to let the little life have its way, with all of God in
nature behind it, a mighty force to turn and overturn all
prearranged plans, or—*kill it!* And the thinking, the plot-
ting, the planning, the efforts that were made in this direction, are a part of the strange history that shall be read in
the day when the books are opened, and shall furnish the
key to the secret of many a ruined home and hope.

Often the little life defies with a strange tenacity all at-
tacks upon it, and comes forth into the great world to ver-

ify the words of Christ that "there is nothing covered, that shall not be revealed; neither hid, that shall not be known. Therefore whatsoever ye have spoken in darkness shall be heard in the light; and that which ye have spoken in the ear in closets shall be proclaimed upon the housetops." The secret wish and purpose, uttered in the motive of the heart, repeated in the murderous efforts of the closet, are published abroad in the reckless, criminal life of the child.

Recently there was brought to my knowledge the case of a mother who reaped the fruit of such designs upon the lives of her children in the suicide, one after the other, of the entire flock; she made the confession at last out of the unspeakable anguish that the abortion had brought to her. There is terrible proof of the need that this subject be agitated by the teachers of this day.

I carry with me a little book that has, among many others, the name of a young married woman who was converted in my meetings and became very active in the church of her choice. She was intelligent, somewhat accomplished, attractive, and soon began to be looked upon as a valuable acquisition to the church society and its activities. But in the midst of her career as a Christian worker there came the summons to retire to the seclusion of her own home, to make ready for the advent of the child that she had asked of God.

With the most ingenuous confidence in the leading woman in the church, she gave her holy secret to her keeping, telling her that for this cause she must be excused from some of the many things expected of her. She talked as a true, loving Christian woman, filled with the tenderest of plans, would talk to an older sister. She expected sympathetic congratulations, but received instead an indignant remonstrance. She was informed that she must not allow *that* to take her out of her active church life.

"Leave the having of children to those who are fit for nothing else" was the older woman's counsel. She must prevent the course of nature and, at all hazards, remain untrammeled. "That is the way I have always done," explained this false teacher. "I made up my mind in the beginning that children must not interfere with my church work, and so I have none. I have come near dying twice," she confessed, "but any risk is better than to be hampered with children."

This woman was always ill, often almost on the verge of the grave in appearance, and had received a great deal of sympathy; had even been accounted heroic in her efforts to do, in spite of many infirmities—and *this* was the cause! The young wife, the child in Christian experience, received a shock to her faith that was almost fatal; and the woman of much zeal was taught a lesson that she would not soon forget.

The revelations concerning these crimes, which continually come to us in our work; the licentiousness confined within the sacred precincts of the marital relation; and the spirit of *murder* thus begotten with the unwelcome child are so appalling that silence cannot longer be "golden," but is rather black as death. The people must be awakened to the awful consequences upon both the mother and the child and society, if the child escape to the birth, so that the instinct of self-preservation shall come to the aid of an enlightened conscience to restrain man and woman from these sins.